OUT OF DARKNESS

——•——

INTO LIGHT

Lauralee Lindholm

TRILOGY
A WHOLLY OWNED SUBSIDIARY OF **TBN**
PROFESSIONAL PUBLISHING MEETS POWERFUL PROMOTION

Out of Darkness into Light

Trilogy Christian Publishers A Wholly Owned Subsidiary of Trinity Broadcasting Network

2442 Michelle Drive Tustin, CA 92780

Copyright © 2024 by Lauralee Lindholm

All Scripture quotations are taken from the Holy Bible, New International Version®, NIV®. Copyright © 1973, 1978, 1984, 2011 by Biblica, Inc.™ Used by permission of Zondervan. All rights reserved worldwide. www.zondervan.com. The "NIV" and "New International Version" are trademarks registered in the United States Patent and Trademark Office by Biblica, Inc.™

No part of this book may be reproduced, stored in a retrieval system, or transmitted by any means without written permission from the author. All rights reserved. Printed in the USA.

Rights Department, 2442 Michelle Drive, Tustin, CA 92780.

Trilogy Christian Publishing/TBN and colophon are trademarks of Trinity Broadcasting Network.

For information about special discounts for bulk purchases, please contact Trilogy Christian Publishing.

Trilogy Disclaimer: The views and content expressed in this book are those of the author and may not necessarily reflect the views and doctrine of Trilogy Christian Publishing or the Trinity Broadcasting Network.

10 9 8 7 6 5 4 3 2 1

Library of Congress Cataloging-in-Publication Data is available.

ISBN: 979-8-89041-889-0

E-ISBN: 979-8-89041-890-6

Endorsement

I first met Lauralee and Ray Lindholm in the northern highlands of Ethiopia in the early 1970s. Our children were attending the same school at the time, and we were invited to spend the Easter break with the Lindholms and the other Southern Baptist missionaries working in Menz. I was impressed with their dedication, zeal, and unusual approach to reaching out in the context or restriction, challenge and adversity.

Out of Darkness into Light is a book that, once started, I could not put down. It is well-written with good description and anecdotes, a real adventure with real live missionaries. It is a well-told story that moves along in its telling such that the reader has a sense of participating in the journey as it unfolds. It will be shared among friends and read by mission strategists and those seeking to break out of the well-worn and unproductive mission strategies of the past.

I think one of the greatest takeaways is the remarkable, creative approach used in bringing the people they served out of the darkness and into the light. The Lindholms were not building a congregation of their own, but they were building where God was already at work. They did not seek to enrich themselves, but rather they sought to enrich those they served in a creative, life-giving, and self-sustaining way. One of the tests of any work and ministry is what happens after the missionaries leave—and in the case of the Lindholms, they were forced to leave and yet their work remains.

Out of Darkness into Light can be read by anthropologists for the insights into culture and life among these remote Ethiopian people hidden for so long. It can be read by educators and community developers seeking to impact culture with new and innovative ideas, and by missiologists who will note the unusual, multifaceted approach used—working through the ancient Orthodox Church, teaching and training, while providing skills and trades at the same time. The life-changing message of the Gospel flowed openly and smoothly in this approach.

I highly recommend Lauralee Lindholm's book, having observed firsthand the Lindholms' work and ministry as reflected in this story.

Roberta Kells Dorr
Author of THE HOUSE OF DAVID trilogy: *David and Bathsheba*; *Solomon's Song*; *Queen of Sheba*, published by Chosen Books

Dedication

This book is gratefully dedicated to all those in the Great Partnership, without whom this story could never have happened:

- People everywhere who prayed faithfully for us and for awakening in Menz.
- The churches that provided for our needs so we could go.
- The Ethiopian preachers and singers who shared the Gospel on tape in their native tongue of Amharic.
- The missionaries who labored before us, sowing the seed, with little visible fruit.
- The writers who put God's message in print in Amharic tracts and books.
- The dorm parents and teachers at Good Shepherd School, who so willingly cared for and taught our children.
- The pilots of Missionary Aviation Fellowship, who flew us, along with their wives, who stood by on the radio.
- The missionaries stationed in Addis, who took care of things so we could live and work in the countryside.
- The tape preachers who taught and inspired us.
- Our parents, who gave up their children and grandchildren as we answered God's call.
- Our children, who accompanied us to a strange land and shared us with its people.

TABLE OF CONTENTS

INTRODUCTION..................9

THE CALL..................15

THE ORTHODOX..................23

A SIGN..................29

SHAKING OFF THE DUST..................35

A GREAT EAGERNESS..................41

PRAYER POWER..................47

BOOK BURNING..................53

STIRRING UP THE MOBS..................57

MAKING TENTS..................61

REVIVAL..................73

PERSECUTION..................81

THE TRIAL..................85

STRENGTHENING..................93

THE ENEMY..................103

STUMBLING BLOCK..................111

THE INCREASE..................117

THE OUTCASTES..................127

GROWING STRONGER..................137

PROTECTION..................147

Table of Contents Continued

Witnesses..155

The Fire Spreads...161

To the Ends of the Earth..............................171

Arrest..181

Set Apart...189

Epilogue...197

Afterword..199

Translation of Amharic Letters............201

Glossary...205

Introduction

"You're forbidden to go any farther. Go back to the mission house and don't leave it. We'll be checking on you regularly," said the local officials as they turned them back.

Even though they had tried to mentally prepare themselves for this possibility, they still found the official pronouncement came as a shock. Four of them had made the trip: Dr. Jerry Bedsole and Dr. Dale Beighle, veterinarians; Lynn Groce, an agriculturalist; and Muko Okare, an Ethiopian doctor who worked for the mission. They had planned to go on to their homes in Tsahai Sina, sixteen miles farther, but they only made it as far as Mehal Meda, the capital of Menz. They had all pinned such high hopes on this last visit to the area where they had lived and worked for so long.

Several weeks earlier, when the local officials ordered them out of Menz so they wouldn't inadvertently be involved in the escalating war, they had left so hurriedly that they had forgotten some things. Also, they hadn't had a chance to say enough "goodbyes." Now they had a car full of Bibles and some veterinary medicine that they wanted to get out to the people.

Now they were under house arrest, and it seemed obvious they had wasted their efforts. What was worse, they might not be quickly released. It had been only four days since their fellow missionary, Dr. Sam Cannata, had been freed after sixteen days in prison in the capital of Ethiopia, Addis Ababa.

As they dejectedly headed for the house, they went over their plans for the trip once again. They had spent considerable time in prayer over the wisdom of this journey, and all the missionaries, including the wives, had agreed it was the Lord's will that they should go. This assurance gave them little comfort at the moment, however, as they watched an armed guard make a circuit around the house.

Just the day before, the government had called a meeting in the town of all the leaders of surrounding areas. Priest Girma, as chairman of Kaya, was obliged to attend. His three close friends—Tatuk, Girma, and Aschallew—went along to provide him with company.

As the meeting drew to a close, a glance at the sky told them they would have to hurry to make the long, seven-hour walk home before darkness descended. In a race against the sun, they set out at a brisk pace. As they reached the last rise on the outskirts of town, before dropping into the valley below, they heard the faint sound of a car engine. They turned to watch for its approach. As they waited, they began to dare to hope that it might be the missionaries returning. The village hid the car from their sight, but the trail of dust rising led unmistakably to the mission house.

No discussion was needed. Quickly retracing their steps, they ran to find their friends. Kissing each other on both cheeks in traditional greeting, they couldn't help but conclude that God had arranged this meeting. Although the missionaries were forbidden to leave the house, their Ethiopian friends were allowed to spend the night with them. Even the knowledge of their confinement that night didn't quench the joy they felt as they prayed and fellowshipped together.

The young men from Menz were eager to tell of the Lord's work in recent weeks and of the growing thirst for the Bible, which they were attempting to meet. Considering the missionaries' present condition, it was obvious that their return to work in Menz was very unlikely. The young men saw that their time had come. As they talked with the missionaries, the torch was passed.

"Until now you've been teaching us the Bible and sharing Christ with us. We understand that you may have to leave, but God has shown us that we're to share the Gospel just as you have. You can be sure that we'll remain strong in Jesus because of your witness." With these words the young men said goodbye.

Before they left, arrangements were made for these four from Kaya to take with them all the Bibles and medicine that they could carry. They would return later for the rest. The missionaries were allowed to leave on the following day on condition that they return immediately to Addis. Six weeks later, in June 1977, all Southern Baptist missionaries left Ethiopia. We had been there exactly ten years.

In the beginning, when people found out that we intended to work in the back hill country of Menz, they simply clucked their tongues in disbelief and dismay. No foreigners had ever lived there and no person who left ever returned by choice. The most optimistic said that it would be at least ten years before anyone would trust us and become friends.

But the chain of circumstances in our getting permission to work in Ethiopia, and in Menz in particular, dispelled any doubts we might have had. The Lord's leading was plain, and we never seriously considered turning back. The first few years flew by as we struggled to learn Amharic, build our homes, and get a feel for the culture and customs.

Ray Greeting Emperor Haile Selassie

The Ethiopian government gave permission for Southern Baptists to begin work on condition that we establish a community development program in Menz—an almost totally undeveloped area. It was the area of Emperor Haile Selassie's roots, and he was interested in its development. Thus, as missionaries, we began some rather unusual programs: rug weaving classes, bridge building, high altitude crop experimentation, and mobile medical and veterinary clinics.

At the same time, we began to get acquainted with the Ethiopian Orthodox Church in "the oldest Christian empire." Exotic sights, sounds and smells assailed our senses as we attended early morning mass each Sunday. Religious holidays were particularly interesting and colorful. With our increased understanding of the people came a growing love and concern for those so long isolated in a spot time had forgotten.

Because the ten-thousand-foot-high plateau of Menz is cut to ribbons by huge gorges every few miles, the world has passed it by. It remains virtually unchanged from centuries past. Its people live very simply—most just one crop failure away from starvation. A worse threat though, is the danger of being killed or injured in one of the frequent family feuds over land, or by a thieving neighbor.

Menzies live scattered all over the plateau and cliff sides, farming every scrap of arable land. The soil is depleted and is full of rocks. Farmers use oxen and a single spear point plow to till the hard dirt. Little grows at such high altitude except barley, chickpeas, and lentils. Thus, their diet is very simple. The staple of every meal is *injera,* a large thin pancake made of fermented batter. It is always served with *wat,* a sauce that is frequently made of chili pepper or lentils. They also raise chickens, sheep, and cows and on occasion they have meat, eggs, or yogurt. *Tella,* a fermented barley beer, is often served.

Their homes are small round huts with rock and mud walls covered by a thatch roof. A low bench along the outer wall serves as the only furniture. The walls, bench, and floor are plastered periodically with a mixture of animal dung, urine, and straw. The same mix is made into flat cakes that are dried in the sun and are used for cooking fuel. Cooking is done on a fire ring in the center of the room and most homes have no windows because they would let cold air in. As a consequence, most homes are dark and smoky inside. If a family is affluent, they might have a second-story room over their animal shelter with beds made of eucalyptus poles with cowhides stretched tight on them. Several family members often huddle together in each bed for warmth.

There is no electricity and the only light after dusk comes from the wick of a diesel oil lamp—equal to the light of a candle. Water is brought some distance from a spring in big clay pots. Women and girls must trek to the spring every morning to bring the daily ration of water to be used for drinking, cooking, bathing, and washing clothes. It is, of necessity, used very sparingly. There are no outhouses or sewers.

Menz families are almost self-sufficient. What they don't make themselves, they can trade for at the weekly area market. A few traders are always there with items in demand such as rubber shoes or boots, safety pins, salt, and guns. People rarely have more than one change of clothes. They wear a locally woven woolen blanket or a white *gabi* (large cotton shawl) after the sun goes down or on cold days. Men and boys always carry a *doola* to serve as a walking stick and defense weapon. Nearly everyone travels over the rough terrain on foot. For most Menzies, there is virtually no contact with the outside world.

The more we learned, the more we came to appreciate people's comments of skepticism and downright disbelief about the advisability of our mission work in Menz. Yet the Lord displayed his wisdom through our ignorance. In ten years, he accomplished greater things than we dared dream of seeing in a lifetime.

For six years we sowed the seed with no visible harvest. Yet we continued sharing God's word in faith, claiming the promise of Isaiah 55:11 that God's word would not return void, but would bring forth fruit. Then came the first fruits and the battle began. As more of the harvest ripened, the battle raged more fiercely. Each time the enemy sent his fiery darts, the Lord miraculously cared for his own. And with each victory the harvest multiplied, and the body grew a little stronger.

Over and over, we relived the days of Acts with Paul and the disciples as we experienced spiritual warfare in Menz. The testimony of the disciples having been through it before and of God's faithfulness, provided us with strength to stand against the enemy and kept discouragement from overcoming us when things seemed darkest.

God is alive! He has won the victory over Satan through Jesus Christ. He works today as He did two thousand years ago, and this book is a testimony of His hand moving in one small part of the world to bring people out of darkness into light.

Once again God fulfilled His promise in Matthew 4:16: "The people living in darkness have seen a great light; on those living in the land of the shadow of death a light has dawned."

My hope is that this book will encourage believers who are facing persecution today. I trust it will reenergize those who have grown weary or cold in their Christian walk. Above all I pray that any who have not experienced God's love and forgiveness through Jesus Christ will discover it firsthand through this amazing story.

The Call

During the night Paul had a vision of a man of Macedonia standing and begging him, "Come over to Macedonia and help us." After Paul had seen the vision, we got ready at once to leave for Macedonia, concluding that God had called us to preach the gospel to them.

Acts 16:9–10

What next? Again and again, we asked ourselves this question in the fall of 1973 as we waited for the Lord's leading. Ray and I both felt that our ministry would take a different direction on our second tour in Ethiopia. During our first three years we were kept busy as Ray taught rug weaving in the mission handcraft school and I schooled our three children: John, Julie, and Stephen. With all we had to learn, our hands were full and those beginning years passed quickly.

Lindholm Family

Recognizing the crucial importance of fluency in Amharic, we chose to take a four-month refresher course when we returned from furlough. Our tedious hours of study paid off. We were rewarded by being able to go beyond superficial small talk to expressing things of the heart.

Now our children were boarding at Good Shepherd School in Addis Ababa where they stayed during the three terms of the school year. After each term they came home to Menz for a month of vacation. For the first time since our oldest son was born twelve years earlier, just the two of us remained at home.

From the start, our mission stressed mobility—going to the people rather than expecting them to come to us. Medical and veterinary clinics fit in very well with this approach, but handcraft teaching was another matter. It takes a long time to teach a new skill and people need to learn every day, so we hadn't seriously considered it.

We began to weigh the idea of going mobile too. The mission already had a large circus-type tent. If we stayed in one area awhile it just might work. As the idea took root in our minds, we began to wonder where. We asked the Lord to show us the place.

The answer came more quickly than we expected in a way no less clear than Paul's Macedonian call. Within a few days a young man came to our door and introduced himself as Asefa. He told us he had just come from Mehal Meda where he had taken a test to get a job as a guard at a government clinic. As things moved incredibly slowly in Menz, he had to wait in Mehal Meda several months for the results.

To help pass the time, he began going to Bible studies at Dr. Cannata's house. Once his interest was captured, he didn't miss a meeting. Long before he found out that he had passed the test and gotten the job, he discovered Jesus and became a new person. He could hardly contain his excitement as he shared his newfound joy with us. But he had more in mind than just telling us his good news when he stopped by our house.

Asefa wanted us to go to his home area of Kaya and tell his neighbors the same things he had heard at Cannata's house. He was certain that they would come to know Jesus just like he had, once they heard the Bible in their own language. We were a bit skeptical. Although we hadn't yet been to Kaya—an area about twenty miles west of us—we had been preaching and teaching in Menz for four years already. In all that time, not a single person had truly grasped what it really meant to be a believer in Jesus Christ. After making sure we would pray about it, Asefa went back home.

Cannatas came to hold the weekly Thursday clinic the next day and were eager to share with us about their first born-again believer. When we asked if his name might be Asefa, it was their turn to be surprised. Before they left, we prayed together for the Lord's leading in the matter of beginning work in Kaya.

Two days later, Asefa showed up at our house again. This time he had a long sheet of paper covered with writing. A close examination revealed over two hundred laboriously penned signatures in Amharic script. He had decided that the best way to show us that people were willing to learn was to go from compound to compound all over Kaya, getting the names of those promising to come to classes. The list was visible evidence of his faith.

This time we didn't hesitate. We chose the next Saturday to begin our teaching and asked him to spread the news. We briefly considered commuting the forty-mile round trip daily, but the road was little more than a dirt track and the trip usually took an hour—if there was no trouble. Gas was quite expensive, and we had to bring it in barrels from Addis, consequently we rationed it very carefully. Furthermore, the jolting ride left us feeling something like a weary horseman and it took a while to recover.

As if these reasons weren't enough, there was something else that was even more important. We were convinced that the only way we would ever get to really know the people in Kaya was to live among them. After loading our Land Rover and trailer with the big tent, our own camping tent and equipment, enough supplies for a week, plus handcraft teaching tools and Bible study helps, we were set to go.

The Land Rover and Trailer Packed to Go

We found a crowd waiting for us at the appointed spot in Kaya when we drove up. All were eager to help in any way they could. In preparation for setting up the big tent, they had felled two eucalyptus trees as big around as a man's leg and had cut them to the right lengths. Meanwhile we spread out the huge roof canvas on the ground as they enthusiastically pounded stakes around the edge.

Finally, two groups of young men dragged the freshly cut poles in under the canvas and inserted them in the two metal caps in the roof. On the count of three, at Ray's direction, they all pushed on the poles and the tent began to rise. We were as thrilled as they were the first time the big tent went up. None of us had ever seen anything like it before.

The daily classes reached a wide range of people. Due to a very low literacy rate in Menz, nearly everyone was interested in reading, writing, and arithmetic. To help us teach the basics, we hired a young man named Moltote who was born in Menz. He was trained as a child as a deacon in the Orthodox Church but later moved to Addis to go to school. While he was there, he found a living Savior.

Even though he only got as far as the sixth grade, he qualified for the job of teaching beginning literacy and that is what he was doing when we met him. He was excited about returning to his home area to teach and witness to his own people, even though it meant leaving the comforts of city life behind.

Handcraft classes were another regular part of each day's activities. All women in Menz are expert at rolling small wooden hand spindles along their legs to spin cotton and wool. They spend hours preparing to spin by fluffing the fiber with their fingers. It is a tedious and time-consuming labor.

Ray had examined old carding combs in the U.S. and knew that factory-made models would be neither available nor economically feasible in Ethiopia. He was convinced he could make something equally useful that would be affordable. Taking blocks of wood, squares of cured rawhide, and wires from strands of old broken steel cable, he made carding combs. With them the work of hours could be reduced to minutes.

Change, for people who are unaccustomed to it, is a very threatening thing, so we went slowly. Ladies came and spun our wool, first using the carding combs to prepare it. We promised them a set of cards when the course was complete if they wanted them, and most did.

Every two weeks our doctor and vet came for scheduled clinics. Jerry worked with animals in the meadow while Sam took care of people in the tent. Even though all he had with him were some suitcases of medicine, Sam was able to help everyone in some way. Only about one out of twenty couldn't be fairly adequately treated in this inexpensive and simple way, and for them there was hope in the hospitals of Addis.

We also helped in a massive smallpox eradication program as the World Health Organization determined to stamp out the disease once and for all. Menz was the center of the last area in the world to still have cases of smallpox. Due to the rugged terrain and the natural hostility and distrust of the people for strangers, they had a hard time tracking down cases. We were able to help both in giving vaccinations and in reporting fresh outbreaks.

Living right with the people we saw countless ill. For many of them their conditions were chronic, and they had just resigned themselves to living that way. We were glad we could offer them some help. This was really a concrete way of showing them that we cared.

Lynn Groce came regularly, too, and brought seeds to distribute as well as sheep and chickens to sell for breeding purposes. All were sold at just the right price—cheap enough so people could afford them but expensive enough so that they wouldn't want to eat them.

Our biggest drawing card though was our daily film showing. Using a small filmstrip projector that works off a car battery we showed simple Bible stories every evening. Although everyone in Menz is an Orthodox Christian, the old familiar Bible stories were new to all. Word had already reached the country of the wonders of the city—especially of its modern "cinema." When they saw the colorful hand-drawn pictures of people in long robes with bare feet doing all the same things they do every day, they were sure the "cinema" had come to Menz at last. We didn't attempt to destroy the illusion.

With the setting of the sun, people could stop work for the day. They flocked to the big tent. Shepherds hurried to get their sheep safely home so they could come too. Some simply left them outside the tent to graze.

Young and old alike watched transfixed as the evening's story unfolded. The filmstrip was repeated for latecomers and those who didn't grasp everything the first time. The retelling was punctuated with frequent questions to be sure that they got the message. Finally, one of us made a brief application of the film to their lives, challenging them to consider it. Then, before complete darkness fell, we let them go. They quickly scattered to their homes, bolting their doors against the dangers of the night.

The Orthodox

As was his custom, Paul went into the synagogue, and on three Sabbath days he reasoned with them from the Scriptures, explaining and proving that the Messiah had to suffer and rise from the dead. "This Jesus I am proclaiming to you is the Messiah," he said.

Acts 17:2–3

Our boldest step in the tent program was to schedule a Bible class especially for priests and deacons, late on Sunday morning following mass. Although a number of our rug students were priests and deacons, and several others were among our friends, we had never before held a special Bible study just for them. We felt somewhat presumptive when we announced the class, and we wondered in our hearts if any would come. But we couldn't escape the conviction that God was leading us to do it.

Ethiopian Orthodox Christians claim that the Bible is the inspired Word of God. But for most, the only Bible they have ever seen is written in *Ge'ez,* now a dead language in Ethiopia. Its script is the same as Amharic, so they are still able to read it, but the forgotten tongue is meaningless to all but the deepest scholar. They have the Bible in Menz, but they don't know its contents. Consequently, it has no real effect on their lives.

In 1970, the summer after our mission began work in Menz, the Orthodox Church began a Rainy Season Bible School for priests and deacons (young men training for the priesthood). We helped by supplying the textbooks—Bibles in Amharic. Most who attended had never seen a Bible before, and they were very interested. There were still those, however, who were suspicious of anything new. Word quickly spread that this was a "Foreigners' Bible," and it wasn't the same as theirs.

The teacher, a young Orthodox leader from Addis, heard these rumors and tried his best to refute them. But the damage had already been done. Then he had an inspiration. As a large crowd looked on, he marched right into the "Holy of Holies" of nearby St. Mary's church. This is the sacred place where the *Tabot* (Ark of the Covenant) rests—a box covered with a gilt cloth containing the holy books, pictures, and relics that are looked on almost as the soul of the church. Here he found a copy of their *Ge'ez* Bible, which he took out to show the expectant onlookers.

Placing the old Bible beside the new one he alternately read the familiar old *Ge'ez* words and then the new words in Amharic. To all who had some knowledge of *Ge'ez* it was obvious that they were both saying the same thing. As a final, convincing proof, he showed them the picture and endorsement of Emperor Haile Selassie, right on the first page of the new book.

And so they were introduced to the Bible. For many, they only learned enough at that first Rainy Season Bible School to whet their appetites. There were about a dozen students in particular who were really eager to discover what was in the Bible. We didn't know it then, but they "happened" to live in Kaya.

As we waited that first Sunday morning in the tent, wondering if any would come to the Bible study for priests and deacons, those that the Lord had prepared were hurrying our way. The Bible studies were, of necessity, very simple at first. Because it took quite a bit of time to help each one find the place in the unknown book, we concentrated on a single scripture passage for an entire lesson.

Priest and Deacon Bible Class

They asked lots of questions. Since there were no outsiders or church members present, they could ask even the simplest things without losing face. Each knew they weren't alone in their lack of knowledge. They had never been taught the stories and truths of the Bible. The class finished at noon and the afternoon service didn't start until 3 p.m., but many just stayed around during the hours in between. It was during times like this that we began to really get to know them.

Occasionally we stopped to ask ourselves if we were qualified to teach the Bible to priests and deacons. Ray had an M.A. degree in teaching biology, and I had a B.A. degree in Sociology, but we knew that those credentials were of no real value. Beyond that, we did go to Golden Gate Seminary for a year of theological study. But we actually got most of our Bible knowledge day by day and week by week as we grew up in Christian homes. We read the Bible regularly and benefited from many teaching programs in our church.

Every time we got a little timid and faint-hearted, someone would ask us a simple question that we could easily answer. As we saw comprehension dawn, we felt the special blessing that only a teacher can know. Then we were sure once more that it was right for us to be teaching them.

As the disciples went to the Jewish synagogue every Sabbath wherever they were, we attended the Orthodox Church every Sunday. In our attempts to appear inconspicuous and to make them feel more comfortable, we tried to follow their customs as best we could.

Most churches in Menz are large round mud and rock buildings with thatch roofs. Right in the center is the "Holy of Holies" which only priests and deacons can enter. Around it is a circular room where priests perform the mass, carry incense burners and other holy articles, and pass out blessings. Everyone else stands against the outer wall.

As they enter, the women with heads covered go to the right-hand side and men to the left, first taking off their shoes (if they have any) and leaving them neatly outside the door. Inside the women and men are separated by a thin curtain. All stand during the long hours of the mass with the help of a leaning stick—rising and falling whenever appropriate. There are no benches or chairs.

Each church has a patron saint and every month all work stops on the day of their saint in order to give honor. Once a year people come from miles around for a really big celebration in honor of their patron saint. This is an especially festive occasion with much elaborate pageantry. Sometimes on these holidays, if there are visiting dignitaries, there are speeches or a sermon after the lengthy mass.

After we had attended Orthodox services for several years, they commented on something very unusual they had noticed about us. We attended every week. No one but the very old and some of their clergy approached our attendance record. Even priests often stayed home if it wasn't their turn to perform the mass.

From the first, our mission had simple Bible studies or sermons at clinics, the handcraft school, and our homes. Before long we began to be asked to preach outside their churches after mass when we attended on Sunday. Those first sermons in Amharic were quite a struggle and some people just shrugged their shoulders and quit making the effort to understand, assuming that we were speaking in a foreign tongue. But we didn't give up.

After mass and preaching there is usually a memorial service in honor of someone who has died—either a week, a month, a year, or even several years ago. The relatives bring huge thirty-pound loaves of bread and jugs of beer for those gathered. The food is divided, and all must be eaten for the maximum benefit to be received. Each participant says a word of blessing for the deceased. As they got to know us better, they urged us to join them for some of the bread at least. Sitting with them week after week our understanding continued to increase.

We were not welcome at every church by any means. There was a fear of the unknown by many, and some were convinced that the presence of a non-Orthodox foreigner would defile their church. One week word came back to us that if we attended the church at Tudobar we would be stoned. Actually, we never went to any church that hadn't specifically invited us, and in no case would we attend without a church or community leader as escort. So, they needn't have worried.

While in Kaya we alternated going to the two nearest churches, Akafee and Zigba. On our last Sunday there we planned to go to Zigba, but on Thursday our host, a community leader whose land our tent was on, told us to go to Akafee with him. As we thought this over, Priest Girma came and rescinded his invitation to Zigba. We wondered what it all meant and prayed with Moltote about it. Since we didn't feel at peace about going to either place, we stayed home that morning. Later we learned that they had planned to beat us at Zigba if we had gone.

Attendance was good every week at our priest Bible class. At the end of six weeks, we surprised them by giving each regular attendee a Bible. For many it was the first book of any sort that they had ever owned, and they received it with evident pride and joy. Thus, the first seeds were sown, and we claimed the Lord's promise that they would bear fruit.

A Sign

Crispus, the synagogue ruler, and his entire household believed in the Lord.

Acts 18:8

The response to the priest Bible classes was so much greater than we had anticipated that we began to dare to enlarge our dream a little. We had prepared ourselves to wait ten years for a real acceptance among the people and it had been only a little over six since our mission came to Ethiopia in 1967. We really shouldn't expect anything yet. Still the Lord began to kindle a hope in our hearts.

Because our mission approach of working in the Orthodox Church was a rather unusual one, a lot of people were watching closely. Some were sure it would never work and didn't hesitate to tell us so. Others were skeptical but wished us luck. Still others were excited about the prospects and encouraged us in many ways.

As interest in the Bible grew in Kaya, the Lord gave us the vision to pray for a sign. We asked God to stamp his seal of approval on our work with the Orthodox by causing one church leader to recognize Jesus Christ as his savior. As we dared to request this, we were filled with a sense of expectancy.

A few days later Priest Girma came to our tent on a weekday afternoon. The white turban on his head readily identified him as a priest. It was the first time anyone had come alone to talk about the Bible. We found out that although he was only twenty-eight years old, he was the head priest of his church. He had been promoted to the chief position five years earlier when some older priests died, and another had to give up his title because his wife passed away. By Orthodox custom, a priest must be married. If his wife dies, he becomes a monk.

Then he told us an interesting story and we saw once again the intricacies of God's working. To officially enter the priesthood, he had to go to the capital, Addis Ababa, and be anointed by the *Abuna* (Pope). He was but one of many priests from all over Ethiopia who were given the authority of the church that day. After the ceremony the *Abuna* urged each new priest to buy a Bible in Amharic. Since most of them were from the countryside, a majority had never seen a copy of it in their everyday tongue.

A Bible at that time cost $1.25, and in a country where the average annual income is only $100, that was a lot. But for some unexplainable reason, Priest Girma bought one. He didn't know of a single other person who followed the Pope's urgings. Taking it home he began to read—on page one. He found some things he didn't understand. In fact, the farther he read, the more questions he had. But there was no one he could ask or get help from, so he finally just quit reading—until we arrived.

He came to us for explanations, carefully considering both our answers and the Scriptures we showed him. Day after day he returned with deeper and deeper questions. At last, one day he admitted that he was profoundly troubled. Putting it graphically he said, "I feel like a man who has long hair on one half of his head and is shaved on the other side." He was being torn in two directions by habits of a lifetime and by the Lord's spirit working in his heart.

"All my life I've believed that salvation comes through baptism as a baby," he confided. "And all babies are baptized—boys at forty days and girls at eighty. So that means that everyone in Menz is a Christian. But

I've been reading the Bible, and it doesn't say that anywhere—at least not that I can find. Instead, it says that salvation is a gift of God through His grace."

"I also read that it's necessary to repent of one's sins to be saved and I've discovered some new things about sin. As an Orthodox Christian I've always thought that the two most important areas of law keeping were fasting and observing religious holidays."

"You know we fast every Wednesday and Friday and for two months before Easter. Everyone has to avoid eating meat and all animal products such as milk, cheese, butter, and eggs on those days. We, the priests and deacons, can't eat anything until after noon on fast days and on some special holidays we don't eat at all. I've been quite careful about keeping the food laws and my conscience is clear on that subject."

"Then there are religious holidays. Every day of the month is named in honor of a particular saint. Some of the saint's days every Orthodox Christian observes, such as Saint Mary's Day. On other saints' days, only those churches in the immediate vicinity of the church claiming that patron saint keep the holiday."

"For each of these days, there is a long list of rules of things you can and can't do, and everybody knows them by heart. About half of the days of each month we are prohibited from working or can only do certain kinds of work. I try hard not to break the law by doing anything I shouldn't on those days. I know that people watch me very closely since I'm a priest."

"But I discovered something new when I started reading my Bible. It's a set of laws in Exodus called the Ten Commandments. Although we Orthodox observe lots of Old Testament laws, such as what kind of meat to eat and how to properly kill an animal, no one has ever said anything about these ten rules."

"Some seem fair enough, such as not killing. But I found others that surprised me, such as one forbidding lying. You have to lie in Menz, or you'll be cheated. Whenever a person is asked a question, he always lies at first. That way he has room to compromise. After a lot of talk, if the truth is absolutely necessary, you can always swear an oath to show you really mean what you're saying. Of course, even the oath doesn't actually guarantee honesty."

"Then there's the matter of adultery. Adultery is a way of life in Menz. A woman is counted as a good wife only if she can bear children, and one sure way to guarantee a marriage will work is to try her out ahead of time. Also, it's very cold in Menz. A good host always provides his guest with a sleeping partner, and Menz men travel a lot."

"And as if the Ten Commandments weren't enough, Jesus said that even thinking about doing something wrong is sinning. I'm beginning to think I never really knew what sin was before. Up until now, I believed that as long as you receive communion right before you die, your slate will be wiped clean. One of my main jobs as a priest is to try to get to any person who is dying soon enough to give him communion one last time."

"I now see that there is more to it than that. It's necessary not only to confess sin to God but to really repent, which I now realize means to stop doing it. God is the only one who can forgive sin and I don't think he wants us to wait until we're dying to ask Him."

He asked us to pray with him for God to show him what to do and to give him peace in his heart. He understood that he was trying to walk two roads and he had to make a choice. Right after that our time in Kaya ended and we moved back home to our house in Tsahai Sina. Before we left, we gave him "The Road to Salvation"—Book One of our Mission Correspondence Course.

One afternoon about two weeks later, we were surprised to see Priest Girma coming across the meadow. We knew it was at least a three hour walk from Kaya. We wondered what could be important enough to cause him to make the tiring trip. He was clutching the completed study course in his hand, but we suspected that there was more to his visit than that.

He answered our unspoken question immediately. While out reading his Bible and praying under a tree, he made his decision to completely commit his life to Jesus Christ. He poured out his heart to God, acknowledging that he was a sinner. As he experienced God's love and forgiveness, happiness filled him to overflowing. We were thrilled to share the joy of his newfound faith and it was several hours before we said goodbye and he set out for home. God had answered both of our prayers. He found new life, and we got our sign.

Almost immediately we began noticing changes in his life. On Sundays after mass, he began preaching a short sermon at church. When some objected to his not reading "Miracles of Mary" often enough, he didn't argue. Taking the old favorite book, he told them, "You all know who Mary was. She was a young woman chosen by God for a very special task. It was to bear a baby. And do you know who that baby was? It was Jesus, God's Son." And with that introduction, he was off on a sermon that invariably ended with the promise of salvation through Christ.

There were some, of course, who opposed him, but he was not unused to opposition. When he got his Bible five years earlier and began reading it through, he decided to name his two little boys Danael (Daniel) and Yonas (Jonah). Such a thing is unheard of in Menz, and his relatives were incensed. Names reflect family hopes for the child and titles of pride and mastery are the norm, such as, "Rule over them," "My king," and "Push them in the ditch." But Danael and Yonas they remained, living evidence of God's hand on Priest Girma.

Not long after he accepted Christ as Savior, he came again to pray and talk with us. He had a new burden. He was concerned about his wife and sons knowing Jesus. Also, as he performed the mass each week, he began giving new thought to everything he said and did. The service itself was fine, although it was all in *Ge'ez* and no one understood it. But there were some other customs that had developed through tradition, and they were not so good.

Since the day he committed his life to Christ and really tried to live for Him, a lot of people had turned against him. Some had even gone so far as to threaten him and his family, promising harm if he didn't give up his "foreign ways." Opposition was heaviest from some of his fellow church leaders.

As a result, he had reached a sad conclusion. It isn't possible to be a born-again Christian in Menz. The only solution would be to give up his inheritance, leave his relatives and friends, and take his wife and children to a place where there is religious freedom.

Then we shared with him the vision that had kept all of us missionaries going those first six years. We saw Menz as a land of darkness and had been praying that God would send a light. We had specifically prayed for a sign of God's approval of our work with the Orthodox by showing us one born-again believer. God had answered that prayer by placing one small flame in a corner of the darkness.

What a difference that tiny light made! Already it didn't seem as dark. If God could kindle one flame, couldn't we trust Him for more? We could see hope beginning to return as Priest Girma caught hold of our dream. We prayed together that more would have their eyes opened to the truth just as he had.

Shaking Off the Dust

But the Jews incited the God-fearing women of high standing and the leading men of the city. They stirred up persecution against Paul and Barnabas, and expelled them from their region. So they shook the dust from their feet in protest against them and went to Iconium.

Acts 13:50–51

During those early months of the tent ministry, Moltote was our right-hand man. He could see both sides of the picture. Until he was ten, he had lived in Menz and was trained as a deacon. Then he went to Addis to school and found Jesus Christ. Even though he didn't speak any English, when we didn't understand something, he was able to explain it to us within the limited framework of our Amharic. Most importantly, he helped us get to know the culture. Things that happened began to make more sense when we were aware of what lay behind them.

Moltote's coming to Menz was a direct answer to prayer. When we returned from furlough and were studying Amharic in Addis, we began asking God for a Christian helper in Menz. We talked to our friends in Addis to see if they knew of anyone. It was really a big request since we had never met anyone used to city life who voluntarily returned to live in the countryside. School graduates assigned to work in government schools or clinics in Menz literally counted the hours until they could escape the primitive conditions and return to civilization.

Then a friend brought Moltote to us. His father had recently died, and his mother was left alone in Menz. He felt like he should go and help her. Also, he was anxious to share his Christian faith there.

We soon found out that he was an excellent literacy teacher, even with only a sixth-grade education. In addition, we got something we hadn't expected; he turned out to be an inspired preacher. Going everywhere with us, he was frequently asked to share from the Bible. He always had something relevant to say, no matter what the occasion. When either of us spoke, if people had trouble understanding, Moltote was able to make things clear. There was no question in our minds but that God had sent him.

As the three of us prayed together daily for the Lord's work in Menz and in our own lives, we grew very close. He confided one day that since returning to Menz, he had felt "a fire burning in his heart" to lead his people to Jesus. We knew exactly what he meant.

We stayed in Kaya for six weeks, just as we had planned. We knew that everyone had left work undone at home to attend classes and that the time had come for them to return to the fields and their household chores. Folding our tents, we went back to Tsahai Sina. It was nice to enjoy the comforts of home again, but we weren't anxious to stay there for long. We had sensed the Lord's working in Kaya and felt that this might be the beginning of something big. We asked the Lord to show us where he wanted us to go next.

The head priest from Wuhay church came to our home a few days later, pleading with us to go to his area and teach. Wuhay was five miles south of us, across the river. Jerry Bedsole had been teaching on Sundays at Musullah Maryam church nearby, but no one had been to Wuhay itself. We agreed and on the next Saturday, with our trailer loaded to the hilt, we bumped along for forty-five minutes through the river and over plowed fields to the designated area.

When we arrived at what we thought was the spot, no one was there to meet us. Soon, however, a couple of young women we had trained as literacy teachers arrived on the scene. They had been holding classes in Wuhay for about two weeks and were glad we were coming to help them out.

After making sure we were in the right place, we began unloading and setting up. As usual, we set up our own small tent first. Then we tackled the big tent. The first step was to spread out the large canvas that would become the roof. By this time a number of people had shown up to see what was going on. We went on with our work, carefully laying out the poles and ropes in just the right places. Finally, everything was done, and we were ready for the tent raising.

As we were trying to decide what to do next, we spotted a group of priests and deacons coming over the hill. We recognized them from a distance as they were wearing white cloths wrapped neatly around their heads as a sign of their position. We were glad they had come at last so that we could get on with the business of setting up.

As they got closer, we began to suspect that everything was not all right. They were talking loudly back and forth, glancing frequently in our direction. Finally, when they reached us, they demanded to know what we were doing there. We couldn't believe our ears!

We looked around for the priest who had invited us and were relieved to see him coming, a little behind the group. We were sure he would straighten everything out. But as we carefully watched and listened, the truth gradually dawned on us. They were all drunk!

We found out that they had spent the entire morning at church at a *tezcar*—the annual ceremony in honor of someone who has died. The richer and more influential the deceased was, the more food and drink that is brought, and it must all be consumed. Sometimes it takes hours— as on that particular Saturday. The result was plain for all to see. It was obvious that we couldn't expect help from any of them.

We decided to take the matter into our own hands. We urged them all to sit down in a group and to let each one have his say—in an orderly manner instead of all yelling at once. Amazingly, there was no objection.

At last, we found out what the trouble was. Several years earlier, when one of our missionaries built his house, he lived in this same tent during construction. Thus, by logical deduction, they could see the same pattern repeating itself. Today we were only going to set up a tent. But that was just the beginning. Next thing you know, we'd be building a house on their land, and they sure didn't want us to do that.

We were certain that we could explain everything to their satisfaction, now that we knew their misconception. We patiently told them about our plans for the tent program and what we had done in Kaya. Then we talked about our house in Tsahai Sina which most of them had seen. We assured them that one house was enough for us and that we definitely wouldn't build another on their land.

But facts spoke louder than words. They could see the other missionary house from where they were sitting. It was just too big of a risk. How did they know we'd keep our word? It was better not to let us even get a foothold by setting up the tent.

At that point a man jumped up, deciding it was time for action. He ran over and grabbed the tent canvas. Others quickly followed, all trying to get rid of the offending object. As their hands clutched at the old sun-worn canvas, pulling in every direction, it began to rip.

We hastily gathered up everything and threw it in the trailer, not bothering about neat packing this time. The sun was dipping behind the hills as we pulled away from the angry mob. We could tell by their defiant gestures that they felt they had succeeded in ridding their area of something very undesirable.

Sleep didn't come easily that night. We kept wondering what went wrong. Early the next morning we were awakened by a small group of sober and repentant priests. They begged us to reconsider and return at once to Wuhay. But the previous day's experience was still very fresh in our minds. We told them we needed to pray about it.

We suggested that they talk to the others in Wuhay to see if they really wanted us back. If they did, they could come and see us again in a few days. We stressed that it was vital for everyone to settle on a spot for us to set up the tent before we would consider coming back. They reluctantly agreed and retraced their steps back home.

During the next week, the Lord did not give us peace in our hearts about returning there. Consequently, we weren't too surprised when no one came back with arrangements for our coming. It was plain to see that God had closed the door on Wuhay, at least for the time being.

After Christmas, in January 1974, our mission had a four-day prayer retreat. All our missionaries left their work and gathered at a rest camp run by another mission group. We studied the Bible, and as we did, we took time to examine our hearts once again. The Holy Spirit worked in each of us.

We discovered sins we hadn't recognized and areas of our lives that we hadn't fully committed to the Lord. As God moved in our midst, we experienced His presence in an unmistakable way. The fellowship was sweet, and we all grew closer to both the Lord and each other during our days there.

As we prayed for Priest Girma and our friends in Menz, we realized that just praying for a sign wasn't enough. God increased our faith and led us to claim forty people in Menz coming to know Jesus Christ in a real way. We were excited and almost overwhelmed just by the thought of it. But we had a God-given conviction in our hearts that it would happen. We returned to Menz from the retreat, eager to see just how God would do it.

A Great Eagerness

Now the Berean Jews were of more noble character than those in Thessalonica, for they received the message with great eagerness and examined the Scriptures every day to see if what Paul said was true.

Acts 17:11

We got back from the prayer retreat just in time for the biggest religious holiday of the year. The air was alive with excitement as people got out their holiday best.

Timket (Baptism Day), celebrating the baptism of Jesus, falls near the end of January. Virtually everyone in Menz throngs to church on that day, and we were no exception. In the wee hours of the morning the ceremony begins. At first there is only a handful of priests and deacons, but as others come, the service gains momentum. The resonant throb of the drums, coupled with the metallic clack of the shakers, provides the background pulse for the chanting.

Each chant is a little faster and a little louder than the one before as the mass mounts in crescendo. Finally, there isn't room for another person in the packed church. At that precise moment the women show their ecstasy by uttering a shrill high-pitched trill. To us the service seemed not only exotic but hauntingly beautiful.

Elaborate robes and caps are donned by the priests and deacons on this most special of occasions. The rich gilt cloth is of brilliant colors covered with sparkling embroidery and ornaments. Over each priest holding a holy book or cross is held an equally ornate umbrella. The umbrellas are a sign of great honor and reverence. In addition, the priests carry large brass crosses and incense burners.

Orthodox Holiday Celebration

On the most important holidays they bring out the *Tabot* from its resting place in the Holy of Holies. Carefully placing it on the head of an elder priest, they drape a gilt cloth over it, and then an ornate umbrella is held over everything. Some churches have more than one *Tabot*, and each is carried in the same carefully prescribed way.

With the *Tabot* and the priests bearing it at the head of the procession, the rest of the priests and deacons quickly fall in behind. Immediately after them are the men of the countryside, each shouldering an old rifle, forming an unofficial bodyguard. As they march along, they raise their voices, repeating the special song reserved for occasions such as this. In the milling crowd that follows, the young women band together to sing over and over the song that is their part of the ceremony.

The procession is very slow as the priests carrying the *Tabot* in front move with deliberate dignity. If it is at all possible, they go to a spot near water—either a stream or a cliff edge in sight of water. Sometimes it takes hours to reach the chosen destination, but that doesn't dampen their enthusiasm. If you stand a little apart from the throng, you hear an unusual, though not unpleasant, cacophony of sounds.

A small cloth tent awaits their arrival, and the *Tabot* is carefully deposited inside. After another elaborate ceremony, the procession with the *Tabot* still at the front, wends its way back to the church. Once again, the *Tabot* returns to its resting place, and the people go wearily, but happily, back to their homes.

As we mingled with the holiday crowd, we found Priest Girma with a friend who was head priest of a neighboring church. Priest Dugafee had heard about our program in Kaya and was eager for us to come and teach in his area, Aloe. It was immediately to the south of Kaya and seemed like a good possibility to us. He invited us to come to their church on a coming saint's day to explain our program to the people.

Mass was already over when we arrived at the Aloe church, and they were just getting ready to sit down and eat together. All the area leaders were there, both church and community, and they gave us a warm welcome. We ate and talked for two hours, and they were unanimous in asking us to come and teach there.

After eating we started discussing a tent site. Several urged us to live inside a compound so that they could protect everything from thieves, but we weren't anxious to do that. Each compound has at least one dog trained to bite any intruder. I had the unhappy experience one day of feeling a snarling dog clamp his jaws into my ankle just as I stepped into the shelter of a house, thinking I was safe. Fortunately, I was wearing long pants and thick socks, so it didn't break the skin, but it did make me wary of dogs.

Also sewing up dog bites is one of the main jobs at our mission clinic. Because of this, people are hesitant to enter someone else's yard unless they are personally escorted by the owner, and he keeps the dog at bay with his *doola*, or stick.

We wanted people to be free to come and go. We had lived in an open meadow in Kaya, and we only had problems with petty theft when we weren't careful to put things away. We finally convinced them that the Lord would take care of us, and everyone agreed on a central meadow as a camp site.

On arriving we set up the same schedule that had worked so well in Kaya. On Sunday we were happy to see a tent full of new faces at the afternoon Bible study. Just as we were about to begin a group that we hadn't expected showed up. It was the priests and deacons from our previous location in Kaya. They admitted that it was at least a two-hour walk, but that didn't seem to really concern them. As long as it was at all possible to attend the Bible studies, they wanted to come.

Nights are very chilly in Menz. The atmosphere is thin at 10,000 feet, and the wind blows continually. The only sensible place to be when the sun isn't out is in bed. The morning after our big Bible study in Aloe, it was frigid when we awoke, as was typical. The first rays of the morning sun were inching their way toward our tent as we tried to gather courage to make the plunge from our warm beds to our cold clothes.

Just then we heard some unusual noises outside. It sounded like people clearing their throats. Since that's the way you make your presence known when there are no doors to knock on, we asked who they were and what they wanted. In response they stammered apologetically, asking our forgiveness for bothering us at such an early hour.

Their spokesman said, "We know you have classes already planned for today, and you're probably tired after a busy day yesterday, but we wondered if you have a little time to teach us the Bible right now?"

We couldn't believe our ears, but we didn't ask them to repeat their request. Dressing quickly, we invited the priests and deacons from Kaya into the tent. Beginning with prayer, we studied the Bible. As we taught, for our own benefit, we constantly compared the Amharic Bible to our English version. They paid close attention to everything they heard and read. When we finally checked our watches, we were amazed to discover that two hours had passed.

Assuming they probably had work to do, we figured that we should let them go. We closed our Bibles and sat back, indicating we were finished. As they grasped our meaning, looks of disappointment registered on their faces. "Are you tired already?" one of them dared to ask.

Once more, we felt as if our ears were playing tricks on us. They wanted more! So, we opened our Bibles again and the study went on—for two more hours. At this point, we felt certain that they must have had enough. While we were teaching, Moltote had gone ahead and taught literacy in the big tent. Only a smattering of people had come for these classes, so he was easily able to take care of them.

Again, we felt we had to stop and give them a chance to leave. Our hesitancy stemmed from the fact that we had never met anyone who wanted to study the Bible for so long. We were concerned that somehow, they might be feeling like a captive audience. Maybe there was something in their culture that we didn't understand, and they were just too polite to leave.

After four hours we stopped and indicated that they were free to return home. As they struggled to understand our feelings, one asked, "Is that all you know?" That was the only logical explanation he could see for our ending the Bible study.

Convinced at last that they still wanted to learn, we opened our Bibles for a third time. When we noticed the sun's rays were coming from directly overhead, we knew they must be hungry. We suggested stopping so that they could eat lunch. They hurriedly informed us that they had eaten before they set out that morning and they didn't plan to eat again until they got back home in the evening. They had grown accustomed to doing this on long trips or when they were out working in the fields away from home.

At last, we caught on. They wanted to learn all day! When we asked about their farm work, they assured us that they had done all they could until the rains came. They couldn't plow or plant until the ground was good and wet. In the meantime, they wanted to know if they could spend their days of waiting for rain, studying the Bible.

It was something we had dared hope for only in our dreams. Now it was really happening. There were so many things we wanted to teach them, and they all seemed so important. The hours literally flew by that day, and it was sundown before we knew it. But they came back the next day and the next. Our daily literacy and handcraft classes never gained much momentum in Aloe, but the Lord was carefully working out His own plans.

Prayer Power

At Iconium Paul and Barnabas went as usual into the Jewish synagogue. There they spoke so effectively that a great number of Jews and Greeks believed. But the Jews who refused to believe stirred up the other Gentiles and poisoned their minds against the brothers. So Paul and Barnabas spent considerable time there, speaking boldly for the Lord, who confirmed the message of his grace by enabling them to perform signs and wonders. The people of the city were divided; some sided with the Jews, others with the apostles.

Acts 14:1–4

While in Aloe, we attended Priest Dugafee's church with him. We didn't want to offend those worshiping in any way, so we tried to be very observant regarding their customs. Some at the church were quite friendly and helpful—showing us what to do and when to do it. But there were others who were suspicious.

After our second visit to the church there, something unusual happened. Someone stole the *Tabot*. Word spread quickly that the foreigners had not only taken the *Tabot*, but had sold it. We knew denials were futile, so we kept silent. But we quit attending that church.

It wasn't until several weeks after we left Aloe that the *Tabot* reappeared. One of the deacons in the church, evidently resenting our presence, had taken it on himself to remove the *Tabot* and hide it in a cave down on the cliff side to keep it safe. Even his bringing it back didn't remove the stigma from us. The church members were grateful to him for safeguarding it. If he hadn't, they reasoned, we undoubtedly would have stolen it.

We had a compelling desire when we came back from furlough and returned to language study, that somehow God would show those in Menz the power of prayer. We wanted them to know a personal God who is alive today—one who answers prayer and cares about each and every one of us.

Practicing praying in Amharic was a big part of our daily lessons. We found it to be one of the most difficult things we'd ever done. It's one thing to make mistakes in conversation with friends, but it's something else to be tongue-tied before God. We felt painfully self-conscious as we tried to translate our thoughts into words that were awkward and unfamiliar. Finally, after months of practice, came a sense of feeling "at home" in the language and we finally accomplished our goal. We were able to talk to God, as well as to our Ethiopian friends, in Amharic, our adopted tongue.

Now we had been back in Menz for eight months. More than ever, we wanted God to demonstrate that prayer is real in a way that our country friends couldn't fail to grasp. We knew that it would have to be something pretty unusual to catch their attention and convince them.

Those who were around us very much soon discovered that we prayed a lot, and at some rather unusual places. For one thing, we prayed every time we ate, whether at their houses or at ours. Every Bible study, clinic, and handcraft class was begun with prayer. Each time we had a problem or decision to make, we first consulted the Lord.

This kind of spontaneous praying in Amharic was something entirely new to them. What they were familiar with were church prayers. They are the special duty of priests and are all in *Ge'ez*. Since they are carefully and thoroughly memorized, they can be rapidly recited, almost without thought.

Making up a prayer as you go was an almost inconceivable idea for them. They had never thought of it before, but now they heard us doing it. We wanted more than anything to show them that prayer is the way to communicate with God and that he does answer.

Once each week Ray and I returned home from tent living on clinic day for the weekly Thursday yarn and rug market. In addition, we got to take a bath and restock our larder for tent living. While there we took the opportunity to get together with any of our fellow missionaries who were in Menz, to pray and share with them about the Lord's working that week.

Because it was both tiring and time consuming, we didn't take down our small tent and take everything home on Wednesdays. Quite a few people were genuinely concerned about the wisdom of our leaving things behind in our absence. Whenever it was mentioned, we expressed our conviction that God was capable of taking care of what he had given us. As a precaution, we did have a guard provided by the local landowner.

Each week we carefully put everything away and after zipping up the tent, we tied down the flaps. But you can't really lock a tent. When we returned on Thursday afternoons, and we found that all was well, we couldn't help breathing a small sigh of relief, accompanied by a prayer of thanks.

One day we weren't so fortunate. The usual crowd was waiting for us by the tent when we returned after a busy twenty-four hours at home. It was always nice to get back to the slower pace of camping out. Approaching the tent, the first thing that caught our attention was a broken zipper. A hurried glance inside confirmed the worst—somebody or something had gotten inside.

Everything was in a state of complete chaos. We quickly stepped in and unzipped the windows to let in some air. Those outside pressed against the mesh to see for themselves what had happened. The mess was unbelievable. Our food, books, clothes, and teaching supplies were strewn all over. Even the stuffing out of our pillows was loose and was mixed up in the mess.

Our first impression was that it was simply a terrible joke. Maybe someone had opened the tent and some wild dogs had gotten in and torn things up. But those who knew the ways of Menz suspected otherwise.

They began to cry with rhythmic sobs, giving vent to their grief. "We knew it was too good to be true," lamented one. "Now you'll go home and won't ever come back here and teach us again."

Another expressed a common sentiment declaring, "We told you that you shouldn't stay in the meadow, but you said your God would take care of you, so we decided to wait and see. Now we know that we shouldn't have agreed."

While trying to reassure them, we attacked the mess. We noticed that chalk messages had been scribbled all over. They didn't provide any clues, but we knew someone had been in our tent who had learned to write. Finally, everything was back where it belonged. At that point it was obvious that a lot was missing. At our friends' insistence, we began making a list.

Our sleeping bags and coats were gone. With them were the hiking boots my dad had sent for use on steep cross-country trips. The projector and Bible films that were so popular were missing, along with our camera and tape recorder. All our Bibles and study helps were nowhere to be found, and most of our food was either gone or had been ruined. Flashlights, silverware, pots and pans, dishes, literacy supplies, and even my knitting had disappeared. The inventory showed our loss to be more than five hundred dollars.

Once more the people were quick with advice. They said we needed to go to Mehal Meda and take the case to court. That is the standard procedure. The fact that the case drags on interminably and you must spend half of your time there with little hope of satisfaction is considered irrelevant. You're supposed to go. It's the thing to do.

We decided to pray about it. We both felt that the Lord had led us to Aloe and that this wasn't a good time to go away for a long session in court. We reached our decision. We told them that the matter was in God's hands, and we were going to stay there and continue teaching.

For the next two days, people came from all over to commiserate with us. In the midst of it all, God gave us a special blessing—his peace. Even though most of the stuff lost was irreplaceable in Ethiopia, we didn't lose any sleep over it. When people came to cry with us, we were able to comfort them. God was in charge, we assured them. He loved us, and He was taking care of us.

People we had never met before came to see for themselves. With each one we shared a little of Jesus' love. We could see how God was using even the loss of our possessions for his good.

By Saturday things had settled down enough so that we could have Bible studies again. Late in the afternoon, just as we were finishing teaching for the day, a farmer came running our way. He had news for us. He thought he had found our stuff and he wanted us to go and see. Even though it was almost dusk, everyone elected to stay and see if it was true. Nothing could have persuaded them to leave right then.

We got in our car, taking the farmer with us. He directed us to the big community grazing area only a mile away. Right out in plain sight were some familiar looking bundles. The cloth of my coat and our sleeping bags were unmistakable. Without taking the time to untie them, Ray threw them in the back of the Land Rover, and we hurried back to the waiting group.

The rains had finally come, and it had been quite wet for several days, but our things weren't even damp. Obviously, they had been stashed away someplace dry. But if that was the case, why were we getting them back? That question was never answered.

Back at the big tent as we untied and spread out the bundles, everyone gathered around eagerly. Getting out the list, we examined each pile, checking off the items as we found them. Every single thing was there! Even the small change we had received for selling pencils and notebooks wasn't gone. In fact, we found some things we hadn't written down. We hadn't even discovered that they were missing yet.

The people were amazed. They couldn't get over it. One said, "God would do that for you, but he wouldn't for us. You have an 'in' with God that we don't have." The others nodded their heads in mutual agreement.

God had answered our request. He had shown them the power of prayer in a way that none of us would ever forget. We had been telling them about prayer for a long time, but to really be convinced of its effectiveness, they had to see it in action. They had all heard us place our belongings in God's hands and now they were seeing the visible evidence that He had heard and answered.

I think many of them found it hard to sleep that night. I know we did. That proof of God's care for us marked a turning point in the attitudes of many. From then on, they very seriously considered what we had to say.

As for us, we felt like we had received a gift from God. It was above and beyond what we had asked for or expected. We were filled with joy overflowing. As we lay in bed a little later, the events of the day kept tumbling through our minds. We discovered an interesting thing. For us it was a bigger step of faith to accept God's goodness and get our things back than it was to give them up in the first place. We grew a little as we came to understand the extent of God's care for us.

As if all that weren't enough, God still had something else in store for us that weekend. Priest Girma came in the midst of everything, asking a simple question that set in motion a chain of events that would have seemed more in place in the first century than in the twentieth.

Book Burning

A number who had practiced sorcery brought their scrolls together and burned them publicly. When they calculated the value of the scrolls, the total came to fifty thousand drachmas.

Acts 19:19

Seizing a chance to talk to us privately one afternoon, Priest Girma came quickly to the point. "I've been reading Acts," he began, "and it says in chapter 19 that everyone burned their magic books when they believed in Jesus. Do you think that was necessary?"

That was an easy question to answer. We had said repeatedly that it was impossible to serve two masters. If there is any part of your life that belongs to Satan, the Holy Spirit can't dwell there. So, we assured him that what they did was essential.

"That's what I thought," was his immediate reply. "Next Sunday I'd like to bring my magic books and burn them when everybody is there to watch."

We were dumbfounded. Priest Girma was as much as admitting that he was a *tenkway*, or wizard. Just to be absolutely sure, we asked him again. With no attempt to disguise the facts, he answered very simply, "Of course. Didn't you know? I'm the main *tenkway* of this whole area. I quit practicing when I accepted Christ as my Savior, but I still have my magic books at home, and I haven't told anyone of my decision."

Sensing our confusion, he explained further. He told us that he was typical of many who went away from home as boys to learn the mysteries of the church and be trained as deacons. He slept in a small hut in the church yard along with several others his age. The only really adequate meals he got were at memorials for the dead and on church holidays. In between times he was dependent on charity or begging for food.

His deacon training left him little time for much else and his family lived too far away to help. Part-time jobs for pay are something belonging to modern cultures and were unheard of in Menz. Finally, his long apprentice years as a deacon were over. Along with marriage and a family came a chance for the coveted promotion to the priesthood. It is a much-honored position and commands great respect from everyone, but it's also very time-consuming.

By church law, several priests must officiate at every wedding, baptism, and funeral—and these aren't short services. They last for hours and sometimes even days. They are held in people's homes, and country houses are widely scattered. Also, there are countless religious holidays when priests practically live at the church. In short, being a priest is a full-time occupation.

Unfortunately, the salary doesn't match the job. Even the head priest only gets a token payment of a dollar and a half a month. With heavy demands on his time and a family to feed, a priest is forced to look elsewhere for a supplement to his income. And so comes the paradox. The very same man who serves God on Sunday, turns around and gives honor to Satan the rest of the week. It pays very well.

We hadn't been in Menz long before we realized there were men called *tenkways* who played a central role in the lives of the people. We pictured them as wicked, terrible men, and were certain we'd recognize one if we saw him. But we didn't think about it very much since we didn't know any, and it seemed to have little to do with us. Our paths hadn't crossed, and our lives weren't likely to touch—or so we thought.

When Priest Girma told us he was a *tenkway*, we understood for the first time that the Orthodox Church and wizardry are inseparably intertwined in Menz. Most *tenkways* are priests. Because of that, the church doesn't oppose them or speak out against them. There are even more powerful wizards called *dubteras* and they are not incidentally the highest ranking in the local church hierarchy in Menz.

Charms, chants, and ceremonies are all means of paying tribute to the prince of this world, Satan. The *tenkway* has a wealth of painstakingly acquired knowledge and secrets which he uses to tap this evil power. There isn't a person in Menz who hasn't witnessed the dire consequences of defying the *tenkway*, and most are filled with feelings of awe and dread toward him.

The pieces of the puzzle began to fall into place. The bead necklaces that so many wear and the jewelry that no baby is ever without, are not simply for decoration. They are from the *tenkway* and are a means of placating the devil. Also, we had noticed quite a few people with a gold earring in only one ear. Once more we learned that it wasn't accidental, but was a sign that one had a *tzar*, or demon.

Recognizing Satan's power, Menz dwellers have no greater wish than for him to leave them alone. The only way they know to accomplish this, is for one woman in a compound to accept the role of scapegoat. By her willingness to harbor a tzar, or demon, and let him control her, the rest of the family is spared. Because of her sacrifice, they hope to escape sickness, crop failure, disaster, and even death. They know of no one who has refused to honor Satan who hasn't paid dearly for it. The *tenkway* can manipulate the *tzar* and cause it to enter or leave a person. The *tenkway* also prevents hail. The rainy season is always ushered in by sudden violent hailstorms. In an effort to protect their newly sprouted crops, every family in a *tenkway's* area pays him a dollar to put a spell on their land to keep the hail from battering it. Priest Girma could count on ninety dollars twice a year from this job alone. Although he didn't yet have the power to control *tzars*, he was working in that direction—until God turned him about face.

A big crowd had already gathered in the tent on Sunday when Priest Girma came. He rose to speak as we set fire to the pile of wood beside him.

Every eye in the tent was riveted on him as he told of his life as a *tenkway*. Then he shared how God had convicted him of the wrongness of it.

He told them of reading Deuteronomy 18:10–11 and of how it condemned him. It says plainly that anyone who practices black magic, calls on evil spirits for aid, tells fortunes, charms serpents, is a medium or a wizard, or calls out the spirits of the dead, is an object of horror and disgust to the Lord. It couldn't be any plainer. He became convinced that it was impossible to be a *tenkway* and a Christian too.

Because everyone there knew that he was a *tenkway*, he wanted them all to know of his decision to give it up. From now on he was going to trust solely in Jesus Christ. Just then a gasp escaped his spellbound audience, as he pulled out his magic books and flung them into the fire.

The flames licked at the pages, giving everyone time to think. They knew that the missionaries had been claiming that a Christian should trust only in God, and that the devil was already defeated by Jesus Christ. They figured that it was easy for us to say that as foreigners, and they didn't put too much stock in our testimony. After all, we didn't have the same problems they did. We didn't have to deal with the *tenkway*.

Now here was one of their very own priests declaring he was willing to put everything on the line. He was standing against Satan and placing his life in Jesus' hands. A sense of awe and wonder filled the tent. Each one secretly hoped against hope that he would succeed. He had seized the freedom that they longed to have, but what would the consequences be? They would have to wait and see.

News spread like wildfire throughout Kaya about Priest Girma's bold stand. From that moment on, all eyes were on him to see if Satan would retaliate, or if God were really more powerful. The battle lines had been drawn.

Stirring Up the Mobs

When the Jews in Thessalonica learned that Paul was preaching the word of God at Berea, some of them went there too, agitating the crowds and stirring them up.

Acts 17:13

Priest Girma did not turn back. He continued preaching after mass every Sunday to those gathered at his church. They were more tolerant some days than others.

Shortly after he burned his magic books, the time came for his church to celebrate its big annual holiday. Over a thousand people were expected to take part. Thinking about it, he decided that if Menz people were to hear the Gospel, this would be a good place to start, so he set about preparing a sermon. He gave much prayer and deliberation to the words that he would deliver at the time in the service when it was his right as host priest to address the crowd. He knew that they wouldn't be expecting what he had to say and that they disliked change, but he felt that he had to try anyway.

The appointed day dawned clear and beautiful. True to custom, the throng gathered at his church and then made their pilgrimage behind the *Tabot* to a nearby cliff edge and back. As they returned, they anticipated the food they would share. It was an appropriate climax to the much-loved celebration.

Just before the service ended and the *Tabot* vanished once more into its hiding place, Priest Girma rose to speak. The hum of conversation continued, and the people paid little attention to what he was saying. But as they caught snatches of his speech, they realized something unusual was happening. Wondering what was going on, they pricked up their ears.

Now receiving their undivided attention, Priest Girma delivered his carefully-thought-out message with conviction. God's spirit was evident in him as he boldly declared the ageless truth that man is a sinner in need of God. To be sure they understood, he gave some concrete examples—things that were everyday practice among those gathered. At that point he hit home. They realized he was talking about them!

"But there is hope," he continued. "These sins can be forgiven by confessing them to God and believing on Jesus Christ as Savior." The once-silent crowd began to murmur and glance around. Then someone jumped up and began to yell, "We didn't come here to hear all of this! What right does he have to talk to us in this way?"

Confusion broke out all over, making it impossible for Priest Girma to go on speaking, so he sat down. He didn't stay to eat with the others that day. He was very discouraged. Once again, he was convinced that there was no hope for those in Menz. They were too set in their ways. We walked back to his house with him and on the way, we talked. Then we prayed and he decided to try a little longer.

Bad news and rumors travel quickly in Menz, in spite of the fact that there are no telephones and all travel is by foot or on horseback. Reaction to Priest Girma's unprecedented sermon was strong and immediate. Some said we wrote the sermon for him. They were sure he couldn't possibly have done it himself. Most were fairly certain we were paying him. There was no other logical explanation for such a radical change in his life in their minds.

Along with the rumors came threats against him—not just against his own life and property, but also against his wife and children. It became unsafe for him to travel alone or go any significant distance from home.

Meanwhile, Sam Cannata was teaching the Bible to a group of students and government workers in Mehal Meda. Many of them were born again believers. Sam invited Priest Girma over to share his testimony with them.

Most of the students had been raised in Orthodox homes, but when they went to school, they drifted away from the family faith. Education is often accompanied by contempt for the old ways. Thus, students often feel that anything associated with the countryside is backward and should be left behind. Sadly, the Orthodox Church often falls into that category.

They listened to Priest Girma solely out of respect for his office at first. But it wasn't long before they realized that he wasn't a typical country priest. He knew the same savior they did and was a brother in Christ!

After his testimony, they all prayed together and encouraged each other. Their fellowship as believers was a unique combination of joy in their salvation and an excitement about what the Lord was doing. After that visit, Priest Girma didn't feel nearly as alone or discouraged and of the students who heard his testimony, five accepted Christ the next day.

It wasn't long before we heard news of another book burning. This time it was a little different—the book burned was the Bible.

It all began shortly after we moved our tents to Kaya. An imposing old monk came one day with a huge gash in his leg where an angry dog had attacked him. It had been a while since the bite, so it was necessary to clean the area well before applying a dressing. Working carefully but gently, I washed the wound. As I washed, we talked.

He became a monk several years earlier when his wife died. Without his first wife, by church rule, he couldn't continue to be a priest. But by not remarrying, he could still be in the clergy as a monk. Thus, he was now without a home, and he spent his time journeying all over Menz. As he traveled, he preached and taught—particularly at church holidays.

It took quite a while to clean and bandage his wound, so I had ample time to tell him about what we were doing. Before he left, I gave him an Amharic New Testament to add to his prized book collection. His leather book satchel was the only thing he carried in his travels. He seemed genuinely pleased with this new acquisition.

Now, only three months later, we heard that he had burned the New Testament in front of a huge crowd gathered for a church celebration just to the west of Kaya. He said it was a book of the devil. To support his claims, he cited Revelation 1:8, "I am the Alpha and the Omega." Everyone who had ever been to a *tenkway* had heard a jumble of mysterious words. Among them were "Alpha" and "Omega." Both the Bible and the *tenkway* use those same words. What more proof was needed?

Everything said by a church authority is accepted without question by the common people. After all, the leaders are trained in the secrets and wisdom of the church. It is assumed that they know everything about the Bible—both in *Ge'ez* and in the new Amharic translation. If this monk says it's evil, it must be. They were glad he had rid them of this foreign book of the devil.

It looked to us like Satan was marshalling all his forces in counterattack, and he was obviously having some success. He was being forced to defend an area he had held without question for longer than anyone could remember.

Making Tents

*And because he was a tentmaker as they were,
he stayed and worked with them.*

Acts 18:3

With the start of the rains, everyone returned to farming. The rain-softened soil at last yielded to the plow and they could plant. The dried brown countryside was transformed almost overnight as tiny shoots began finding their way to the surface.

It looked to us like we should consider taking down our tents and going home for some time. While we were discussing it, a plane buzzed the tent. We ran out and saw that it was an MAF (Missionary Aviation Fellowship) plane. The pilot circled back and on the next pass a large bag of mail was dropped.

Glancing quickly through the accumulation of several weeks, we found a small note. It was an order for a thousand rugs. The order was unusual, partly because of its size, but also because it was for a different kind of rug from those our weavers had been making.

Ray had been giving some thought to teaching rug weaving in Kaya and that letter settled the issue. As we read it again, we discussed several possibilities. Right then some of the most influential men in Kaya arrived to talk to us. They were seriously interested in helping their people in a concrete way. They had seen the success of the rug weaving project in Tsahai Sina and wondered if we would do something similar in Kaya.

One man had a big compound with several structures in it. One building was never used except to put his animals in when it rained. He offered to let us take it over and use it as a weaving room. So, we made plans to take one young man home with us to train him in weaving this new type of rug. Then he could help us teach the others. We promised to come back in a few weeks.

Before we came to Ethiopia, Ray knew he would be part of a community development team. He also knew that his specific job would be as a handcraft teacher. His only qualifications for that work consisted of a B.A. in history and an M.A. in teaching biology. He had taught for two years in junior high school in the United States and then for three years in a mission high school in Nigeria.

The unique ingredient that fitted him for the job, however, was a lifetime habit of analyzing how things work, making something out of seemingly useless scrap materials, and refusing to admit an item couldn't be repaired until he tried it himself. He has a knack for being able to see the basic elements of anything he looks at without being distracted by the nonessential parts.

As Ray learned about Menz—the area of Ethiopia where we would be working—he found that everybody owned sheep. They are raised for their meat, but an equally valuable by-product is their wool. Menz women are reputed to be the best spinners in Ethiopia, and they use only a simple wooden drop spindle. It's tediously slow but they know no other way.

This handspun wool was used largely to make thick woven blankets that shut out the crisp mountain air. With an over-abundance of blankets on the market, the profit margin for the weavers and wool-spinners was slim.

In the city, they had another use for the wool. They used it to weave rugs. Several handcraft schools produced lovely thick carpets in a variety of traditional Ethiopian designs. The rugs were woven on large looms right in the schools and a new student could enter only when someone else quit. Because of the detailed work involved and the carefully regulated market, these rugs were quite expensive.

Having been raised in the western United States, we were familiar with the beautiful rugs of the Navajo Indians. Before going to Ethiopia, we traveled through their territory and spent some time watching a weaver as he worked. Ray was particularly interested in the mechanics of his weaving, such as the stringing of the loom and the preparation of the fiber.

He found some books on the subject and read them very carefully, mentally visualizing each process as it was described. By the time we arrived in Ethiopia, he knew quite a lot about weaving. With this background, he visited the handcraft schools in Addis and compared their products.

While Ethiopian carpets look very different from Navajo rugs, due to their thick pile, the basic principles of weaving are the same. As Ray observed them, he began to wonder if some of the things they always did were actually necessary. He also doubted that the equipment had to be as expensive and complex as they made it.

When we first got to Ethiopia, we studied Amharic in Addis while the mission handcraft school was being built in Menz. A large rug loom of the three-hundred-dollar variety used in the city, was bought and assembled in a room of the school. Meanwhile, we moved to Menz, finished language study, and supervised the building of our house. A year after our arrival in Ethiopia, Ray was ready to begin teaching his first class of weavers.

Rug weaving, as such, had never been heard of in Menz before we came. They were familiar with cloth weaving though, and there were many skilled weavers in our area. When we opened our handcraft school, our first problem was in finding any students.

The people were openly skeptical about the new venture. They figured it would take a lot of time and most likely no one would ever make any money at it. Thus, we had no volunteers. The problem was solved for us by the man who got us into Menz in the first place—*Ato* (Mr.) Gebre Hiwet, legal advisor to Princess Tenagne-Werk.

He felt that the people most in need of a steady income were the priests and deacons, since they received so little from the church. Firmly convinced of this, he came to Menz, and with the advice of the local head priest, he personally selected the first group of weavers. The school opened with twenty-five students. They came not because they wanted to, but because he said they had to.

At that point, Ray was just as much a beginner as a teacher as they were as weavers. So, they learned together. Making rug designs was also something brand new for Ray, but it had to be done and there was no one else to do it. On those first rugs he tried geometric patterns as well as designs of sheep, lions, churches, and slogans.

Students Weaving Rugs

Some of the original rugs are still around today. They have about as much artistry and beauty as a first-grader's scribbles. But at the time, we regarded them with great pride. Our students were actually weaving rugs!

Before long, Ray tried an Ethiopian cross design on a rug. It was exactly right. Their crosses are famous for their beauty and there are endless varieties in design originating in the many country provinces. Ray adapted several different cross forms into rug patterns.

Along with the improvement in design went a developing skill in weaving. The faster they wove, the better the rugs looked. Ray found that eucalyptus trees from their yards, plus rope and pipe from a plumbing shop, together formed a perfectly good loom—and it only cost fifteen dollars.

The first class graduated, and each weaver set up a loom in his own home. Getting students for a second class was no problem since they could see the first weavers earning money. Again, we stuck largely to priests and deacons. We felt that if our mission was to make any impression on the Orthodox Church, it was good for us to work with the church leaders. Also, we believed in Paul's tent-making principle of a religious leader being able to earn his own keep.

Each day, we had a Bible study and as they got acquainted with the Amharic Bible, we learned its vocabulary. It was a two-way process. They asked questions about what the Bible said, and we became familiar with what they believed.

Before our first three-year tour was over, we had a thriving rug business going. All weaving was now done in their homes, and Ray was frequently called on to visit them to help fix looms or give advice. Some had looms large enough to make room-size rugs. A typical rug market included a wide variety of sizes and designs.

Weekly Rug Market

Our main responsibility in the business after they finished learning to weave, was to buy the rugs and take them to town to our mission headquarters where they were sold. Along with a growing market in Addis, we began getting export orders from several parts of the world. After the first year, the project was self-supporting, with funds for each month's market coming from the previous month's sales.

Things were going smoothly in the rug business when we got the order for a thousand rugs. But this time they wanted the flat weave variety made in northern Ethiopia. Most of those we had seen were not very attractive and were carelessly made. Since no effort is made at quality control on the open market, Ray knew he could teach his students to weave a better rug.

We began our Kaya weaving class in the building we had been offered. Eighteen students were chosen from several different nearby churches. About half of them were the same ones who had been studying the Bible so eagerly.

It didn't take long for them to acquire the basic skills. Then it was just a matter of time until their hands became deft at weaving. We had a Bible study each afternoon, but one day they asked if we would read the Bible to them while they wove. They listened attentively and interrupted only when they wanted something repeated or if they didn't understand.

A big problem was that they were totally unfamiliar with the Bible. When we had Bible studies, we had to find the verse for each one in their Amharic version. After giving the problem some serious thought, we realized it had been solved years before. The answer was in what we call sword drills—group competition in finding books of the Bible quickly.

We passed out lists of the books of the Bible in Amharic. After memorizing the list and reciting it without error, they practiced finding the books. Then when they thought they were ready, we gave them a test. If they could find any book in the New Testament in fifteen seconds or less and tell us what came before and after it without looking, we awarded them a prize New Testament. Mastery of the Old Testament books entitled them to a complete Bible.

As soon as several of them had won Bibles, we let them compete. Every Sunday afternoon, after our meeting, they lined up in the yard by the weaving room. Then I called out the names of books of the Bible. Like children, they could hardly contain their excitement when they located what they were looking for. According to the rules, they were supposed to take just one step forward with their finger on the book name when they found it. In their great fervor, however, they felt that one step was too tame for such a great feat. They preferred to run several steps or shout *Yeehow* (Here it is). It made for lively sword drills.

Students and Sword Drills

We had an additional Bible teaching tool. It was the tape recorder. Amharic preaching and singing were recorded on cassettes in our mission recording studio in Addis. We maintained a lending library of tapes, plus a dozen recorders that we kept in circulation among those seriously interested in Bible study.

For the first time in their lives, they heard fluent preaching and singing in Amharic by evangelical Christians. It wasn't always easy to keep the tape recorders working and keep track of who had them, but it was worth the trouble. A number of them learned to preach and sing from those tapes.

John Cheyne Loaning Tape Recorder to Priest

The rains that began before we left Aloe, continued for several weeks. But on the exact day that we moved back to Kaya to begin weaving classes, they stopped completely. The people had gambled the rains would continue and had planted their grain. It had already sprouted. If it stayed dry too long, everything would die, and they would have no crops. To make matters worse, they would have no seed grain for future planting either.

First, they took the *Tabot* out of the church and prayed to God for rain. Next, they went to the *tenkway*. Still no rain came. Then someone remembered that it had stopped raining when we set up the big tent in Kaya. The tent was still up, and it hadn't rained since. Obviously there must be a connection.

The compound where we were living and teaching was on a steep cliff side above a valley. We parked our car at the top and carried our supplies down the hill each week. One day a friend came and told us we had better move the car. He had overheard some people who were angry about our presence. They were planning to push it over the cliff.

It took an hour to drive back around the head of the valley, along the other side, and down through the creek to bring our Land Rover near the compound. But after it was done, we could keep an eye on our car, and there was nowhere it could be pushed.

The next day the rain came. It was ushered in by a deluge of hail that blanketed the ground like snow, nearly caving in our tent as it collected on the roof. Water gushed down the hillside, its progress checked only by the fence along the lower edge of the compound where we were camped. Soon our tent was completely afloat.

Seeing our predicament, some of the weavers rushed out of the shelter of the weaving room and clawed holes in the rock wall to let the water through while Ray dug trenches. The crisis was averted. That ended the rumors about the tent keeping the rain away, and we didn't have any more threats about our car.

Clutching their recently won Bibles one Sunday, a group of deacons from Akafee went to church. After mass they tried to read to the people from the New Testament. Those attending were incensed and ran them off with *doolas*—the combination weapon and walking stick no Menzie is ever without. They were forced to conclude that the time wasn't yet right to introduce God's word to their church.

Things were getting more exciting by the day. We had Bible studies all week long in the weaving room as they worked, and then had a big meeting on Sunday. More and more of them were coming to talk to us privately and prize Bibles were in great demand. Tape recorders found a ready hearing everywhere they were played.

But we still had only one born again believer. We felt sure the Lord was working in the hearts of these young men who had considered themselves Christians since infancy. But how could we know for sure? We had no way of finding out what they were thinking. We decided we should have a revival meeting. The newly completed community development hall in Mehal Meda was available for our use. Our mission had provided the windows and doors for it. We planned a six-day meeting since many came long distances and we were accustomed to weeklong revival meetings in America.

We were filled with expectancy as the day of the meeting drew near. We had no real way of knowing if anyone would come. We had invited those who attended our Bible studies as well as the priests and deacons from the ten churches that our missionaries went to on a regular basis. As we issued the invitation, they listened politely, but gave no outward indication of their feelings or intentions. Meanwhile we went ahead with preparations for fifty—just in case.

Revival

"Therefore let all Israel be assured of this: God has made this Jesus, whom you crucified, both Lord and Messiah." When the people heard this, they were cut to the heart and said to Peter and the other apostles, "Brothers, what shall we do?" Peter replied, "Repent and be baptized, every one of you, in the name of Jesus Christ for the forgiveness of your sins. And you will receive the gift of the Holy Spirit."

Acts 2:36–38

With preparations at last complete, the awaited day finally arrived. Women in Ginny Cannata's Bible class had spent a busy week getting the food ready. Barley was bought at the market and taken to the town mill to be ground into flour. A cow was brought to Cannata's compound where it was blessed and killed in the prescribed way by a priest. Then it was butchered, and the meat was hung to dry.

Hay was taken to the community hall and strewn on the floor at one end to make sleeping quarters. Negussie Tefera, the evangelist whom everybody was familiar with as a voice on tape, and John Cheyne, one of our missionaries, both came from Addis for the meeting.

On Sunday evening, sixty-five priests and deacons arrived as boarders for the week. The next morning their number swelled to almost one hundred with the addition of those living near enough to commute each day. Attendance was even better than we had hoped.

We scheduled something for every hour of the day. Activities included preaching, teaching, filmstrips, flipcharts, sword drills, Bible memory work, discussion groups, question-and-answer periods, and singing. Between the six of us, we were able to provide leadership from dawn until midnight every day.

We invited the townspeople to come to a service at 5 p.m. daily. Students and government workers crowded the hall to capacity at these times. We began with the singing of gospel songs in Amharic. The students loved singing and the hall resounded with their voices. Our Orthodox friends had never heard singing like this before, and they were both pleased and intrigued. With the printed words in hand, they did their best to sing along.

One of the biggest attractions of the meeting was a sword drill contest between the Orthodox priests and deacons who had been studying in Kaya, and the students who attended classes at Dr. Cannata's house. Most of them were in high school and when they first heard the contest suggested several weeks before the meeting, they thought it was a joke. They were sure that with their superior education, they would easily win any race in finding books of the Bible. When at last Dr. Cannata convinced them that he was serious, they began practicing in earnest.

When the time for the drill arrived, the participants lined up to face the audience. The town crowd was confident that their friends would win with no trouble, until they saw the priests and deacons in action. There were groups from five churches strong enough to compete, plus the students. The first night we had elimination rounds. The students beat everyone they competed against, but so did the deacons from Akafee.

The next night the two groups came face-to-face. Everyone had seen both teams in action and they knew at this point that it would be a close contest. Their speed in locating books was amazing, and many would have found it hard to believe how quick they were if they hadn't seen it with their own eyes.

To win the drill, a team had to get the most points in two out of three rounds. A round was finished as soon as one team reached ten points. The students were good and succeeded in finding some books first, but they weren't good enough. The deacons from Kaya won every round. They were the undisputed champions. None of them had ever been to school and they frequently felt inferior when they were with public school students—but not on that evening.

Finally, the preliminaries were over, and it was time for the message. John Cheyne and Negussie each preached a full-length sermon every night. Although they prepared their messages independently, it was obvious that the same Spirit was directing both of them. They spoke clearly and to the point, and the people were gripped by what they heard.

We made certain to finish before 7 p.m. The hall emptied quickly as everyone rushed home so that they would get there before dark. Then we fed the priests and deacons who were spending the night. They divided into groups of four around large *mesobes* (hand-woven baskets). We parceled out *injera*, a huge cold sourdough type of pancake that is the staple of every meal, and some *wet*, a sauce that is often very hot, plus cooked beef chunks. Several cups of tea and a piece of fruit completed the meal. Talk and laughter came easily as they relaxed after a very full day, and we shared in the fellowship with them. Finally, everyone was served, and we had a chance to sit down around a basket ourselves.

Our program for the day was finished, but the best was yet to come. Each evening following supper, we settled down on the hay for a time of informal discussion lead by Negussie. He knew his Bible inside and out and was obviously led of the Lord in his answers. It was a brand-new experience for our country friends to find a fellow Ethiopian who knew as much about the Bible as the missionaries. They were excited and challenged, and they couldn't hear him enough.

On Wednesday at the close of the late afternoon service, we invited all who wanted to learn more, or who were requesting special prayer, to stay. We knew it would soon be dark out, and it was time to close the meeting.

Every other evening, they had all been very anxious to leave while there was still enough light to show the way home.

Closing with prayer, we indicated that the meeting was over for the day, and all who wanted could leave. Surprisingly, no one moved. Obviously, they hadn't understood. As was often the case, we had probably made some error in our Amharic, so we told them again. This time we made every effort to be absolutely grammatically correct, so that they couldn't possibly misunderstand. Still, no one moved. Losing confidence in our language ability, we asked Negussie to tell them. So, he did—very carefully. Still, they continued to sit expectantly.

At last, it dawned on us that we were the ones who didn't understand, not they. All of them wanted to hear more. So, Negussie explained again what it means to admit you are a sinner. Once you have done that, you need to ask God to forgive you. Nothing else is necessary because Jesus has paid the price already. After a closing prayer the group was again dismissed—but not before we made arrangements for any who wanted to, to talk to Negussie or a missionary the next day.

After supper, we asked Priest Girma if he would like to share his testimony with the evening group of priests and deacons. He said he had been praying about it and although he was still a little nervous, he wanted to do it. He, too, felt that this was the right time.

The group listened attentively, their eyes fixed on him as he spoke. They had never heard anything like what he was saying, and they didn't want to miss a single word. He told of becoming convinced that wizardry was a sin and of how he had totally renounced it. By burning his magic books, he had cast his life completely on Jesus Christ. Three months had passed since his brave action and Satan had not been able to touch him. God was faithfully protecting him. The Holy Spirit guided Priest Girma as he spoke, and his testimony touched the hearts of many. When he finished, after nearly an hour, they were silent and thoughtful. They had a lot to consider.

Earlier in the day, when the afternoon service finally broke up, we had promised to teach all who wanted to learn how to pray. Now seemed to be the right time. First, we defined prayer. We explained that it is simply talking with God. It is not a one-way conversation, but it involves both talking and listening. Using a concrete example they could easily grasp, we compared God to a good father. He is pleased when His children come to Him with their problems and tell Him about them. Because He loves them, He wants to help. Naturally He is happy when they thank Him for His answers.

A father provides his children with food, clothing, and shelter—everything they need. He can't help but be disappointed when they talk to each other and forget about him. He could make them talk to him, but he doesn't want to. He prefers they come to him voluntarily because they love him, not because they have to do so. It's right and good for us to talk to our heavenly Father, just as we do to our earthly father.

All the leaders who were accustomed to praying in Amharic scattered around the room. Then we encouraged the rest to join us. Most did—either out of curiosity or out of a sincere desire to know God better. To give them an opportunity to talk to God, we bowed our heads and had a time of prayer. For the very first time, many of them talked to the God they had spent a lifetime trying to serve, but whom they had never really known.

The Holy Spirit moved in the hearts of many that night and gave them the courage to take this first step of faith. Speaking hesitantly at first, they gained confidence when they found no ridicule or opposition. They thanked God for what this meeting had meant to them already.

The prayer time ended on a note of expectancy. It was obvious the Lord was working. Sleep didn't come easily that night. It had been such an exciting day. We wondered what was in store for us the next day. We felt it might be even greater.

We weren't disappointed. As is usually the case, a preacher or teacher warms to a responsive audience. All the messages of the day were guided by the Spirit and squarely met the needs of those gathered there.

Because most of the priests and deacons had come from the countryside and rarely had an opportunity to visit the town and its stores, we decided to give them the afternoon off on Thursday. Instead of thanks, however, we got complaints. They said that they had only six days to learn, and they could go shopping some other time. They didn't want any time off, so we formed discussion groups for those who wanted to stay.

Just as we got going well, a man came in. He entered talking loudly and argumentatively. Conversation was impossible, for he was obviously drunk. Sam Cannata came over and tried to reason with him, but finally he had to resort to a threat. If the man didn't quit disturbing our meeting, we would call the police.

No sooner had he spoken those words than a policeman walked through the door. The drunk man took one look, turned on his heels, and fled. The policeman, unaware of the drama going on around him, took his hand out of his pocket and showed Sam a bandaged finger. Sam had treated it earlier and had asked him to check back in a week. Since the community hall was near the police station, he decided to drop in there. We were quite sure that his arrival at that exact moment was not accidental.

That evening, as we again settled down in the hay for our nightly discussion, we felt it was time to give them a chance to speak. We asked all who wanted to share anything that God had laid on their hearts that week, to raise their hands. We wondered if any would respond, or if they did, if what they said would be either meaningful or relevant.

To our surprise, nearly every hand in the room went up. By tradition, they let the oldest monk have the floor first. He didn't waste words but came right to the point. The Lord had convicted him of many sins in his life, and he wanted to confess them and find God's forgiveness. His testimony paved the way for others to admit burdens that were weighing heavily on their hearts.

It was May 1974. Ray and I had been in Ethiopia for five years by then, and our Amharic was getting a lot better. But they listed some sins that night we've never needed to know the words for, either before or since. We did understand enough, though, to hear every single one of the Ten Commandments mentioned. Adultery and thievery were common sins, and we even heard murder brought up—and these men were the best ones in Menz! As soon as one person finished, another jumped up in his place to confess and ask God's forgiveness.

About midnight they began to sing. As they sang the old familiar chants from the Psalms in *Ge'ez*, they looked up the translations in their Amharic Bibles. When they read them, they were thrilled by the messages they conveyed. While one beat the drum, the others raised their voices in praise to a God who loved them enough to send his son as Savior. They sang for hours, making some of the most beautiful music we've ever heard.

The night wasn't long enough for everyone to say all that was on their hearts, but they made a good beginning. Finally, with dawn approaching, they settled down for a few hours' sleep. Early the next morning, a large number of priests and deacons were called away to a funeral in Tsahai Sina. We were thankful that it hadn't happened sooner and that they had been there the night before.

That afternoon another drunk came, belligerently demanding answers to questions that don't have clear answers in the Bible, such as "Where was Moses buried?" While he was inside arguing and shouting, another group arrived outside. They were the leaders of the *Baite Kehinet*, the Orthodox council in Mehal Meda responsible for all churches in Menz. Their job is to serve as liaison between the *Abuna* in Addis and the country churches.

They came demanding to know who had given us the authority to hold this meeting. Realizing from the start that it might be a problem, Sam had discussed the proposed meeting with two priests from their office several weeks earlier. Then unexpectedly they were called away from Menz and hadn't been around for the last two weeks. We felt as if the Lord had taken care of the matter.

As they challenged us, the Lord again intervened. The drunk heard the discussion outside and ran out to see what was going on. Quickly switching sides, he began to shout in opposition to those from the *Baite Kehinet* and in our defense. He ran them off and then lost interest and disappeared. Things became quiet again, and we were able to go on with our discussion groups.

The wonderful experience of the previous night did not repeat itself. Many left during the day Friday, and there were a lot of distractions and interruptions as we gathered in the evening. That taught us anew that you can't predict God's working. The best we can do is make ourselves ready and available so that when he does act, we won't miss the opportunity.

On Saturday morning, we had one last Bible study before they left. The group who had shared so much together found it hard to say goodbye. Many of them went home different persons from when they came six days earlier.

We drove home to Tsahai Sina, praising the Lord all the way for His wonderful work. We were full to overflowing with all the blessings He had poured out on us. The awakening in Menz that we had prayed for so long, had at last become a reality. The forces of Satan had been dealt a death blow.

But the devil doesn't give up easily. He fought back with every weapon he had, and he struck while the iron was hot, only a few days after the meeting.

Persecution

But they could not stand up against the wisdom the Spirit gave him as he spoke. Then they secretly persuaded some men to say, "We have heard Stephen speak blasphemous words against Moses and against God." So they stirred up the people and the elders and the teachers of the law. They seized Stephen and brought him before the Sanhedrin. They produced false witnesses, who testified, "This fellow never stops speaking against this holy place and against the law. For we have heard him say that this Jesus of Nazareth will destroy this place and change the customs Moses handed down to us."

Acts 6:10–14

Rumors about the meeting started circulating within forty-eight hours after it was over. Many of the priests and deacons who hadn't attended were suspicious of those who had. No one had been forbidden to attend, so if they wanted to find them at fault, they would have to charge them with something else. Then they had an inspiration. They hit on the perfect accusation.

Word spread quickly that we had fed them donkey meat at the meeting. *Donkey meat*—nothing could have been worse. Because donkeys don't have cloven hooves, they are listed as forbidden animals in the Old Testament food laws. The Orthodox meticulously follow many Jewish food laws and this one is unquestioned. They can't even touch a dead donkey, much less eat one.

In their way of thinking, eating or touching something unholy or defiled makes you defiled. So, they were barred from attending their churches. They could no longer take part in the mass or perform their priestly duties. They were, in effect, excommunicated. Their only recourse was to confess this terrible sin and repent. Then they could be rebaptized and reinstated in their churches. While rebaptism is considered a heresy in itself, it's the lesser of two evils in comparison to eating donkey meat.

There were plenty of witnesses willing to testify against us. One man said that he had seen us kill the donkeys at our house in Tsahai Sina and then take the meat to Mehal Meda. Another said he had taken a picture of Ray killing a donkey, but the picture never materialized. Still another witness said that he had seen Sam killing the donkeys and burying their heads in his yard.

Most people weren't bothered by the conflicting testimony. The word of one person was enough to convince them that the law had been broken. After all, where there's smoke, there's fire. They felt it was important to keep these defiled men out of their holy churches. Five of the ten churches represented at the meeting expelled those who had attended.

Their neighbors and friends began to regard them with suspicion and distrust. Some of them were threatened with bodily harm on the *amudgway*, the big community grazing area between Tsahai Sina and Kaya. For months they had to do all their traveling in large groups for safety.

They could have taken the easy way out and admitted guilt, and the matter would have been dropped. But they knew we hadn't fed them donkey meat. They trusted us and were sure that we wouldn't deceive them. They saw that we were always careful to observe their food laws when we were with them. The new believers realized that the issue at stake was bigger than donkey meat. It was an attack by Satan, and they stood their ground.

Right while this was happening, another problem came up. Every year, at just this time in May, each compound sacrificed a black lamb to Satan. This special sheep was called the *borenticha*. By paying their dues to Satan with this sacrifice, they hoped to avert harm to their crops and animals, as well as to the life and health of their family members.

Once the ritual was complete, they could relax and celebrate. Everyone eagerly anticipated this occasion because it was one of the few times when they had all the meat they could eat. But in order for the ritual to be effective, it was required that every single family member take part.

One of the sins of which God convicted those at the Mehal Meda meeting was the sin of eating meat offered to idols. To them the *borenticha* represented an idol, and they felt that as born-again Christians, they couldn't take part in the ceremony.

Scarcely a week after the meeting, it was time for the sacrifice. As brand-new believers, they were forced to make a choice. They either had to stand up for what they believed or compromise. Realizing it would be difficult, they chose the right course. They refused to take part, much to the consternation of their families. That would displease Satan, and the spell wouldn't work. Some were put under such heavy pressure to take part that they had to either participate or be kicked out of their homes.

Still, they didn't back down or deny their convictions. Those that were thrown out by their families had to find someplace else to stay. But God proved sufficient for each one and they were sustained through these trials.

Not long after the big meeting, they came to us asking us to teach them to sing. They liked the songs they had heard in Mehal Meda. Because they already sang chants in their churches, we had been hesitant to introduce anything new to their culture. Now that they were asking, though, we went ahead and taught them one of the songs they had heard. As all their church songs are in *Ge'ez*, it was a new experience for them to sing in their everyday language of Amharic. They liked the words and their message.

They had all been through years of training as deacons in which they memorized lengthy intricate chants for mass. These are sung either as solos or by several people at once. Although the general pattern of a chant is the same each time, each singer makes his own variations in the tune. Thus, even though everyone is singing the same chant, it doesn't resemble unison, since they aren't all singing the exact same thing.

It was a real hurdle to convey the idea that in singing a tune, there is not only a definite pattern, but it should be sung the same way each time by every person. Alternately, with me singing a line and them repeating it after me, we practiced one song over and over. Whenever I stopped, thinking they had surely sung enough, one would say, "Let's sing it again."

I'm sure we sang that song fifty times on the first day. At last, they were doing a fair job of singing the words together at the same tempo on the same notes, and the song was recognizable. They were so thrilled with their accomplishment. No sooner had they learned that song than they wanted to try another.

A week after the Mehal Meda meeting, a group of those who had been expelled from their churches came to see us at our house late one afternoon. They were pretty discouraged. Not only was the church opposing them, but their families were as well, because they refused to eat the *borenticha*. And so, we read Acts together and they saw how the disciples were persecuted again and again. But the record also showed that God was faithful and was never far from them. We prayed and studied the Bible late into the night and then they rolled up in their blankets and went to sleep on the rug. They returned to Kaya much encouraged the next day.

While we were concerning ourselves about our Ethiopian friends and all the difficulties they were running into, there was trouble brewing for us too. Some discontented people thought they saw a way to get rid of these troublesome foreigners once and for all.

The Trial

Paul wanted to appear before the crowd, but the disciples would not let him. Even some of the officials of the province, friends of Paul, sent him a message begging him not to venture into the theater. The assembly was in confusion: Some were shouting one thing, some another. Most of the people did not even know why they were there. The Jews in the crowd pushed Alexander to the front, and they shouted instructions to him. He motioned for silence in order to make a defense before the people. But when they realized he was a Jew, they all shouted in unison for about two hours: "Great is Artemis of the Ephesians!"

Acts 19:30–34 NIV

Threats were soon directed our way. Anxious friends came to warn us that there were some who were intent on burning down the Cannatas' house. Others threatened to destroy the mission plane—our lifeline to Menz. Members of one church were outspoken enough to say they would stone Sam's car if he came near their vicinity.

We were accused of committing a variety of crimes. The fact that there was a total lack of supporting evidence had little bearing on the rumors. Tension mounted for two weeks until finally a trial was scheduled. Although we were never officially notified as to specific charges, we did receive a summons as defendants. The accused were the three missionary families living in Menz at the time.

We met together the next day when the Cannatas came over for the clinic. Our conversation and thoughts revolved around the latest turn of events. As we talked about the impending trial, we began to hope that it might be an opportunity to tell some important people why we had come to Menz. We knew the Bible promised Paul the opportunity to give his testimony before kings, with words supplied by the Holy Spirit. We prayed that the Lord would be able to use us in the same way when we went to court.

We returned to Kaya in the afternoon for one last meeting before the trial. Twice enroute we found piles of large stones blocking the road and we had to make our way around them, but we finally got there.

Our new family of believers discussed the situation with us. They keenly felt the burden of what we were facing. Their hearts ached to help us somehow. Several offered to go along and fight for us, but that didn't seem like the right thing to do. We felt we couldn't defeat Satan using his own tactics. This battle was God's, and He was in charge of the strategy.

We read from Acts that evening and the next morning. Then before we left, we prayed together again. Lastly, we took down our tents and loaded everything in our Land Rover. Tears were in the eyes of our friends as they waved goodbye, but we felt an assurance that the matter was in God's hands and that He would win the victory.

We drove past our house and on to Mehal Meda, where the Bedsoles and the Cannatas were already waiting. Some influential friends advised us not to go to the trial as they were afraid for our safety. They asked us to wait at the Cannatas' house. If it was alright for us to come, they would let us know.

The government school was dismissed at noon, and most of the nine hundred students eagerly flocked to the unprecedented meeting. The town virtually closed down as everyone crowded into the community hall. There was much speculation as to the outcome, and everyone wanted to see for himself.

Meanwhile we sat marking time at the Cannatas'. It soon became apparent that we weren't going to get the opportunity to witness to those in authority, or even say a single word in our own defense. We could do nothing to help ourselves. All we could do was pray and trust in the Lord to defend us. And that is exactly what we did all during the long hours of that afternoon.

Just as the sun sank, we saw signs of life returning to the town. The first ones to reach us were school kids. We asked them how it went. The only response we got was a shrug of the shoulders and a quick aversion of their eyes to the ground.

Next, some of Cannata's Bible students came by. They provided little more information, except to say that it was bad. We were familiar with the Ethiopian custom that the bearer of bad news must be older or more important than the one whom he is informing. So, we understood that so far no one had felt worthy to tell us what we were so anxious to know.

Finally, the government community development worker, who had been our friend for a long time, came and filled us in on all the details. It came as no surprise to us that we had been accused of stealing the arks from five churches. The impossibility of such a feat without a helicopter, due to the rugged Menz terrain, wasn't even brought up. There were some who willingly testified that the cassette tapes we were loaning out were, in reality, propaganda against the Orthodox Church and its customs. Others said that we were preaching against the church.

There were only a few men at the trial actively making accusations and most of them were people who had complaints against the government or other important men in Menz. They saw a chance to avenge their grievances at our expense. Their real complaints had nothing to do with us.

Some people tried to testify on our behalf, but as soon as one of them stood up to speak, everyone else began shouting at once and drowned him out. One judge spoke out in our favor and was immediately accused of being paid by the mission. Even though there was absolutely no basis for that charge, it resulted in his testimony being completely discredited. Another man who tried to defend us barely escaped being beaten.

The meeting stretched on for five hours before they reached a verdict. According to the consensus, a petition was made out. It asked all the missionaries to leave Menz as soon as possible. Everyone there was encouraged to sign it.

Even though we'd tried to prepare ourselves for the worst, the decision was a blow. We were being asked to leave Menz just when we'd begun to feel comfortable in the language and the awakening that we had been praying for these seven years had at last become a reality. Surely this wasn't the right time to leave.

We debated fighting the decree. It was only semiofficial, because it hadn't been a properly conducted trial. But as we talked it over and prayed about it, we felt we shouldn't resist. God was still in control. Just the day before the trial we had listened to a tape together on all things working together for good for those who love God. We really believed that promise. Here was a chance to prove it.

With the matter settled in our minds, we returned home. Even though it was late in the evening when we arrived, we found sleep slow in coming. Our dreams shattered, we made plans to leave Menz, realizing that we might never be allowed to come back.

The next afternoon some of our friends came to see us. They were very discouraged. Their hopes had been dashed along with ours. They speculated on the wisdom of our attending church the next day. Maybe it wouldn't be safe. They weren't too sure of the mood of the people.

Sunday was Pentecost Day, a holiday. The crowd at church was bigger than usual. We arrived just as the mass was finishing. There was no trouble, and afterwards, a group of about fifty priests and deacons went with us to the community hall across the road for Bible study. They were unusually attentive.

After teaching the lesson, we distributed the first book of our mission correspondence course to everyone who wanted a copy. It gives scripture references and carefully explains the way to receive salvation through Jesus. Almost everyone took a copy. They also wanted help in learning the books of the Bible.

In the afternoon, we drove to Kaya for our weekly meeting. We took one of our workers along as a guard in case anyone felt like pushing our car off the cliff. A much bigger crowd than usual was waiting for us when we drove up.

At first, all they could talk about was the trial. But after we had hashed it over thoroughly, their attention returned to the Bible, and we had an especially good study. Then we had a prayer time, asking, in particular, that the Lord's will be done in the situation.

We had a large escort back up the hill when it was time to leave. It was very hard to say goodbye as we didn't know if we'd be able to come back. A small group of the most faithful believers just couldn't bear to part on that note. They remained after the others left and asked if they could go to Tsahai Sina with us for more prayer.

Packed in our car, they sang the Amharic chorus, "Is anything impossible for God?" over and over all the way home. When we got there, we found more friends waiting at our house. Together we prayed and found comfort in the Lord's promises until midnight. Then we gathered around our table and shared bread and tea. There was a close bond between us as we ate together.

After eating, they stretched out on the couch and chairs as well as on the rug in order to get a few hours of sleep. At dawn we began praying again. Priests and deacons came from all over on Monday and we had prayer and Bible study with each group. Those from Kaya witnessed repeatedly to those who came during the day. In between times they took advantage of their presence with us to learn another song.

On Tuesday, there was another big public meeting. This time it was held in the community hall in Tsahai Sina. People traveled miles from every direction to attend. Once again, we were not included, but we heard the reports quickly this time because the news was good. In an orderly manner, a variety of people told of the ways the missionaries had helped them. After listing all the benefits we had brought to them, they took time to consider what it would be like to return to life as it was before we came.

As they were meeting, the community development officer and some of his fellow workers passed through Tsahai Sina on their way to the government sheep station. Noticing a huge crowd assembled at the community hall, they stopped to investigate. Thus, they arrived accidentally at the meeting, but the people were convinced that God had sent them there.

At the conclusion of the discussion, another petition was circulated—this time asking that we be allowed to stay. It was signed unanimously. On top of that, they chose representatives to go to the authorities in Mehal Meda, the Ministry of Education and the *Baite Kahinet* in Addis Ababa, and even to the emperor if necessary.

Right after the meeting, everyone came to tell us the good news. They were convinced that it was God's work, and they were quick to praise Him. But the original decree still stood, and it was time for us to leave. In spite of the fact that we were being forced out of Menz, there was a feeling among our friends that God would surely call us back. One evidence of this was that three of those who gave false testimony in Mehal Meda had already changed their stories.

After lengthy goodbyes, everyone left at last, and we spent the night loading our car with a few of our most precious possessions and some camping equipment. The next morning, as exiles from Menz, we drove into Addis.

Bedsoles soon left Ethiopia on a regular furlough, about a month ahead of schedule. Boarding school was just letting out for the summer and so we decided, along with the Cannatas, to take our vacations immediately instead of in July as planned. A month should be long enough for us to see what direction things were heading in Menz.

We drove together to Kenya, and the trip provided a much-needed change of pace and a time to be together with our children, but we didn't enjoy it as much as we might have. Always in the back of our minds was the question of whether we'd get to return to Menz or not. Arriving back at our mission headquarters in Addis four weeks later, the first thing we wanted to know was the news from Menz. They had something wonderful to tell us.

About two weeks after we left for Kenya, a delegation of sixteen men made the long bus ride to town from Menz. They each brought petitions filled with signatures. Not only were they from areas where we had mission work, but there were even some from places in Menz where we had never been. They had heard of our work and wanted us to come to each of their areas.

As representatives, they presented a letter to our mission inviting us back to work in Menz. It was the first official document of that nature from the people in authority that our mission had ever received. Those missionaries present in Addis when the delegation came expressed the willingness of our mission to cooperate and then served tea.

On hearing all of this, we didn't waste any time but went straight to Menz the next day. We were welcomed back with a warmth and acceptance we had never felt before. People came from everywhere to hug and kiss us. To show their love, they brought us hundreds of eggs. Over and over, they praised God for bringing us back.

At the time of our trial, *Ato* Gebre Hiwet, the man who had initially gotten us into Menz, was in a hospital in Israel, and he didn't return until the end of the summer. Up to that point, a lot of people had tolerated our presence simply because they respected him, and he had ordered them to accept us. Whenever we had any difficulties in Menz, he was always the one to smooth things out. Now we had to manage without his aid. For the first time we were evaluated solely on our own merits. The people in Menz liked what they saw, and they sent a delegation to Addis to ask us to come back.

Five months later, *Ato* Gebre Hiwet was arrested as a friend of the old government and was put in prison for eight years. At that point we saw God's wisdom. If our presence in Menz had still been based on his authority, we probably would have been asked to leave at that time. But because God knows everything, He had carefully planned so that our mission work was able to go on uninterrupted in spite of political changes. The trial, which had seemed such a disaster at the time, accomplished something that couldn't have come about in any other way.

Strengthening

While Gallio was proconsul of Achaia, the Jews of Corinth made a united attack on Paul and brought him to the place of judgment. "This man," they charged, "is persuading the people to worship God in ways contrary to the law." Just as Paul was about to speak, Gallio said to them, "If you Jews were making a complaint about some misdemeanor or serious crime, it would be reasonable for me to listen to you. But since it involves questions about words and names and your own law—settle the matter yourselves. I will not be a judge of such things." So he drove them off.

Acts 18:12–16

The Kaya believers were still barred from attending their churches, and they continued to be the target of threats. Then one day they received a summons to court in Mehal Meda. They were accused of taking the *Tabot* from their church and selling it to the missionaries two years earlier. No one considered the fact that they didn't even know us then. They were compelled to go to court to defend themselves.

The trip from Kaya to Mehal Meda and back can be made in a single day on foot, but it's very difficult. Usually, people allow two days for the round trip. Our friends had to take precious time from their farming to go and answer the summons on the specified day. When they got there, their accuser didn't even bother to show up, so they were given another date to reappear.

A second time they made the long journey, and once more it was futile. The case couldn't be heard without both parties being present and their accuser had again neglected to come. Their hearing was again postponed.

When they made the trip for the third time, they knew it would be the last. By law, you can only be called three times in a single case. When they arrived, they found the matter had been put in the hands of the governor of Menz. In court, he read over the accusations to familiarize himself with the case. When he saw that they were not accused of breaking any law, he threw the whole case out, saying that he had no jurisdiction over such things. In addition, the accuser failed to come a third time, ensuring that those from Kaya couldn't be called back again on that issue.

The rainy season began as usual in June, and everyone turned to plowing. Several weeks of backbreaking work followed as they hitched their oxen to a single-blade plow and drove them to make furrows in the hard rocky soil. They hurried to get their seed planted quickly in order to take maximum advantage of growing time. In July, the Rainy Season Bible School was held near our home once again. Two Orthodox teachers were brought from Addis to lead it and we helped them in a variety of ways. Country life is always a pretty big adjustment for anyone raised in the city.

At church on Sunday, one of the teachers preached on 1 Corinthians 13. He declared that what is needed most in the church is love and people looking to Jesus. Then he went on to declare that obeying all the church rules is useless without love. When the other teacher got up to preach, he seconded everything the first teacher said.

Those coming from long distances to the Bible school spent the whole week there. They brought their food with them and were provided with a place to sleep. Some of the families of the new believers didn't want them to come and learn the Bible, so they refused to give them any food for the week. It was really hard for those students to find enough to eat, but their fellow believers were faithful in sharing what they had.

Those from Kaya who had been expelled from their churches were among those who came to the Bible school. They made the trek to Tsahai Sina each Monday morning and returned home on Friday afternoon. August marked the three-month point of their exile. They were trying to be patient, but they still wanted to be back in their churches. Then they got an idea that they thought might prove helpful. They asked the two teachers from Addis if they would go to Kaya with them and talk to the Orthodox Church leaders.

That same day, the man who had been most vehement in accusing us at the trial came to ask us a favor. His wife was very sick, and he wanted Ray to take Muko to see her, since she was too ill to be brought to the clinic. It was the middle of the rainy season, and the dirt track that served as a road was almost impassable. Even with four-wheel drive, mud tires, and chains, it is very difficult to go anywhere. If you travel at all, you're inviting trouble.

But the man was desperate in his pleading. If the doctor didn't come, his wife would probably die. So, Ray agreed to take Muko to see her. He could drop off the Bible school teachers in Kaya on his way to the man's house. They were to spend the night in Kaya and return on foot the next day along with the students from there.

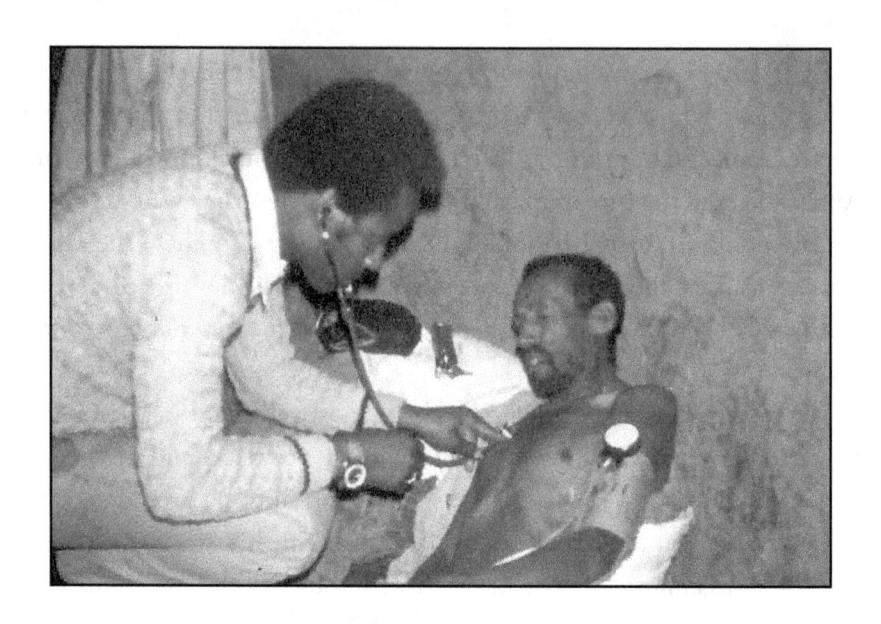

Muko Examining Patient

Ray escaped getting stuck, and Muko was able to give the woman a much-needed shot of penicillin. Afterward, over coffee and bread, they all had a good chance to visit together. The man, who had so vehemently opposed us, now urged us to come and teach in his area. He had been upset with us before because we had been teaching in another part of Kaya, living on the land of one of his rivals. Ray returned home after promising that we would consider the invitation.

A discouraged band of teachers and students trudged back to Tsahai Sina on Sunday afternoon. They had gone to church in the morning, but they had been driven off before they even set foot in the church compound. Those who ran out to meet them shouted that they didn't want the Bible taught at their church. To make sure their message was clear, they took their *doolas* and beat the visiting teachers and those who had brought them, chasing them all away. As they recounted the story to us, the teachers still found such behavior at a church hard to believe, but they couldn't argue with the evidence.

Following the failure of the Addis teachers to aid them in getting back into their churches, they decided it would help to talk over their problem with the governor. A group of seven young men from Kaya went to see him. Since we were going to Mehal Meda ourselves, we gave them a ride. After getting out of the Land Rover, they headed for the governor's office. They hadn't gotten far when one of the men who had been most vocal at our trial accosted them. He menacingly told them that if they went to the governor, he would see to it that they never were able to live at home peacefully again. He would attack them when they were out on the *amudgway*. There was no way they could go anywhere without crossing that wide, barren grazing land.

Filled with fear of him and his power, they dared to see the governor anyway. As they were standing there talking to him, the man who had threatened them was brought in and thrown in jail. A guard at the prison had overheard his words and had reported him. Two other people also volunteered as witnesses against him. The tables were suddenly turned as he found himself locked up.

Those from Kaya had planned to return to the Bible school in Tsahai Sina as soon as they saw the governor, since they had tests the next day. But to make the man's imprisonment legal, they needed to prefer charges. The governor asked them to please stay and do that the next morning.

They knew it would be time-consuming, and they didn't really want to be involved in a court case, but they felt they owed it to the governor, since he was trying to help them. They remained in Mehal Meda and were waiting at the door when the court offices opened the next morning. It still took the entire day to make out, sign, and swear to all of the necessary papers, however. At times they had the impression that they were the ones who were accused.

The final outcome was that the case didn't have to go to court. Their assailant signed a statement that he wouldn't prevent them from going to church or threaten them further. If he broke his word, the police would have the right to throw him back in jail.

The governor decreed that they could legally go back to their churches. It seemed the battle was won. When they got back to their home area the next day, the news had reached there ahead of them. In response to it, the people had changed their strategy and had thought of a new way to oppose them.

They suggested that if any of those accused of eating donkey meat attempted to go to church, everyone else was to boycott it and stay away. Nothing had really changed. They were still, in effect, exiles. There was one difference now, though. There were a number of friends supporting them.

The Bible school graduation was less formal than usual that year. It didn't begin with mass at the local church because the priests hadn't been paid their wages and were on strike. Instead, they asked Ray to preach to everyone and then we gave out prize Bibles to all who had passed the test and had been faithful in attendance.

The Bible school was barely over when Priest Girma came with some startling news. The *Baite Kahinet* in Menz had chosen to promote him to the position of head Bible teacher for all of Kaya and the surrounding area. What a wonderful opportunity! But it turned out that there was more to it than that. His promotion was dependent on his attending Priest School in Addis Ababa for a year. The new class was to begin the following week. He had to make his decision quickly.

The thought of his leaving Menz was a real blow to us. He was the natural leader of the group of new believers. Before his conversion, he had been teaching wizardry to a group of young men who were deacons in the Orthodox Church. Now he was the one those same deacons turned to for strength and guidance in their growth as believers in Christ. He had many opportunities to witness. We were certain we would have a hard time getting along without him.

He was also very concerned about leaving his wife and two young sons for such a long time. But he really did want to be the Bible teacher for the area, and he also wanted more Bible training. He decided to go to Addis and see what it was all about. Then he would make up his mind.

After he got there and investigated, he chose to stay. Each month when we went to Addis to visit our children at boarding school and get supplies, we went to visit Priest Girma. We had so much to share on those brief visits. He was eager for every bit of news from Menz about his family and fellow believers. He was so lonesome for all of them. A time of prayer and sharing together always strengthened the three of us.

Others from the Priest School in Addis started noticing our visits. They came and talked to us, and some sat in on our prayer sessions. As we got to know them, they began to ask if we would come and teach where they lived too.

Priest Girma was eager to learn all he could about the Bible. Most of his daily classes were on church history and Orthodox tradition. He soon began looking for places where he could hear the Bible preached. He found an evangelical church not too far from where he was staying. They had good Sunday school lessons and preaching, and he could make it there in time after he attended early morning mass.

In addition, the headquarters for training soldiers was right next door to the Priest School. He met some of the soldiers and they began asking him questions about the Bible in regard to the Orthodox faith. He was glad for the opportunity to talk to them, and he soon had a regular group of friends that he witnessed to. Knowing they might be called to war at any time, they were very concerned about the real issues in life.

That fall, we were asked to begin a weekly Bible study at Maryam church in Tsahai Sina, close to our house. We had attended mass there more than any place else and Ray was frequently asked to preach when we were there. We had been praying for nearly a year that they would invite us to teach there on Sundays, with their blessing and approval. Then one Sunday the head priest made an announcement to all who had come to church. He informed them that they all needed to know more about the Bible, and he told them that we were the ones who could teach them. Interest was high and from the start we had a big group nearly every time we met.

In addition to this study, we still went to Kaya on Sunday afternoons to meet with a group in the rug room. The profit margin on the flat weave rugs wasn't large enough to make them feasible, so we were now retraining those students to weave the thick pile rugs that had proved such a success before. Our best weaver from Tsahai Sina moved to Kaya to be their teacher, and we went down to work with him a couple of days each week.

A government schoolteacher who lived near us invited us to lead a Bible study on Wednesday evenings in his quarters. A room full of teachers and students gathered there every week. We soon found ourselves having more opportunities to teach the Bible than we would have dreamed possible a year earlier.

When we started teaching weaving in Kaya, our daily classes soon became concentrated on handcrafts and Bible teaching. Since we no longer needed Moltote as a literacy teacher, he was trained by Jerry Bedsole to help him with the veterinary work. In his new role, Moltote still kept busy preaching and teaching everywhere he went.

One of the things that all the believers loved to do was to sing. From the start, we learned Amharic songs along with them as we taught them. Their favorites—the ones they learned most easily—were the indigenous songs which were written in Ethiopia. Ethiopian music is based on the oriental five note scale that produces a somewhat minor sound to western ears. After we grew accustomed to their songs, though, we came to appreciate the beauty that they had.

In Addis Ababa, we were introduced to a book of Orthodox songs that had been translated from *Ge'ez* into Amharic. We got acquainted with one of the singers on the Orthodox Mission radio program in Addis, and he offered to sing them for us on tape. He recorded many of the songs from the book and we used the tape along with the book to teach the believers in Menz. Some of these songs became familiar favorites.

At last, in December, after a total of six months had elapsed, the deacons who had been at the Mehal Meda meeting were allowed back in their churches. The passage of time had accomplished what nothing else could and their long months of waiting had been well spent.

During that time, they had grown into a close-knit body of believers. Each week they met for Bible study and in between times they listened to tapes. They were getting firmly grounded in Bible knowledge. They had learned to sing and now had quite a repertoire of songs. They met often for prayer, and they were witnesses to God's working.

When they finally resumed service in their churches, they were prepared to preach and witness. As persecution so often does, instead of extinguishing the fire, it had only fanned the flames. The fire had grown to the point where it couldn't easily be snuffed out.

The Enemy

Once when we were going to the place of prayer, we were met by a female slave who had a spirit by which she predicted the future. She earned a great deal of money for her owners by fortune-telling. She followed Paul and the rest of us, shouting, "These men are servants of the Most High God, who are telling you the way to be saved." She kept this up for many days. Finally Paul became so annoyed that he turned around and said to the spirit, "In the name of Jesus Christ I command you to come out of her!"
At that moment the spirit left her.

Acts 16:16–18

Priest Girma was the first *tenkway* that we ever knew in Menz, and we had already lived there six years when we met him. But once we became aware of the grip that Satan had on the people through *tenkways*, we saw more and more evidence of their influence.

One man who came to the Mehal Meda meeting openly admitted that he was a *tenkway*. He listened to the testimony of Priest Girma and others as they denounced their former practice of wizardry, and he was moved to action. First, he told those gathered that he was a slave of Satan. It began when he became possessed by a demon five years earlier. At that time, he changed his name to one reflecting his condition. Since it is common belief that demons live in water, he chose the name *Bahiray*, meaning "my sea."

In his years as a *tenkway*, he participated in countless rituals of sacrifice to the devil. He wore a *chulay* around his neck to appease Satan. There are many kinds of *chulays*, but his was a small leather pouch with a piece of parchment inside. When it was unrolled, its length was equal to his height. Incantations were painstakingly etched on it, and all who saw it around his neck knew who his master was.

He had numerous books and charms in his home that he used in plying his trade for all who came to him. As the meeting progressed, he became aware of a freedom among those attending that he didn't have. He wanted to share in it, and he came to us requesting prayer.

He asked what he had to do to have Christ in his heart. First, he would have to repent of his sin of wizardry and give it up, we told him. That meant getting rid of his charms and magic books and putting his faith completely in Jesus Christ. We showed him in the Bible how the devil was defeated by Christ and challenged him to let Jesus do the same thing in his life.

Wistfully he considered it. It was too big a step to be taken lightly. He took off his *chulay* and handed it to us. Then he asked us to pray for him, but he didn't find the courage to commit himself that day. He said he needed to think about it a little more. Several times after that meeting, he came to Sam Cannata's and talked to him, but he was never able to turn his back on Satan and take the leap of faith of trusting in Christ instead.

Our children went off to Addis for school each year. All five of us looked forward to vacations when they came home, as well as to our trips to town during the school year to see them. By far the easiest way to travel was by plane, although it was a little difficult when we were the only missionaries in Menz. That meant we had no one to take us to the airstrip.

We scheduled an early morning trip to town on Thanksgiving Day to spend the holiday with our children and the mission family. Because our Tsahai Sina strip had been temporarily shut down pending removal of all the clumps of weeds on the runway, we had to make the hourlong trip to the Mehal Meda strip. Ray deposited me, along with our baggage, beside the strip and then took our car to the Cannatas' house two miles away. He hurried back on foot to await the plane.

The time came and passed for the plane to arrive and still it didn't come. We waited and waited. It was more than an hour overdue. We didn't dare go back to the Cannatas' to check with MAF on the shortwave radio. If it came while we were gone, we'd miss it. The planes are always heavily scheduled, and pilots can't afford unnecessary delays anywhere. So, we continued our vigil.

At last, we saw a familiar dot in the southern sky. As it grew larger, we detected the whine of the engine. Before touching down, the pilot buzzed low over the strip to be sure all was well. Satisfied, after circling, he landed. Since he was behind schedule, he didn't waste time on small talk but quickly loaded us and our baggage. He promised to explain his delay enroute. He said that he had a very strange story he wanted to tell us. He was still finding it hard to believe himself. Soon we were airborne, and he began his tale.

When he taxied out on the main airstrip in Addis that morning, he had had only a single passenger—a twelve-year-old boy from Menz with leprosy. Sam had sent him to the leprosy hospital in Addis as his case was rather advanced and he needed extensive treatment. He wore special shoes to protect his insensitive feet, and he moved clumsily with considerable difficulty. Because of his disease, he was fragile and small for his age.

After the pilot taxied out on the main strip at Bole Airport, in position for takeoff, the boy signaled that he had to go to the bathroom. The pilot figured that he had better let him, so he parked the plane at the edge of the pavement. The instant the door was opened, the boy bolted. He jumped out and began dashing down the airstrip. Since it is Ethiopia's largest airport, there was plenty of traffic. Our pilot quickly reported his problem on the radio to the control tower, and then took off running after the boy. He figured it would only take him a few minutes, considering his superior size and physical condition.

But he couldn't catch the boy. When the men in the control tower saw his predicament, they alerted the airport fire department. They sent their whole crew out after him. The pilot and the firemen all tried to catch the elusive boy. As they watched him, they couldn't believe their eyes. He ran like a gazelle, back and forth across the strip, easily avoiding their every maneuver. It took more than an hour to capture him so that the airport could resume normal operations.

He was taken to the fire department for safekeeping, and the pilot went on his scheduled flight to Menz without him. As he told us the story, he was still incredulous that the crippled child with the deformed feet had outrun him.

When we arrived at the airport, we had to go and get the boy and take him back to the leprosy hospital. He would have to wait until another day for a ride to Menz. I went to get the car while Ray headed on foot to the fire department. I met them on the road and found them chatting happily. Since I was already at the wheel, Ray settled the boy in the backseat and got in beside him. We talked about familiar Menz things on the way to the mission compound, which was next door to the leprosy hospital. He seemed happy and relaxed.

About a mile from the mission, we crossed a small stream. At that moment he went berserk and began shrieking and howling. He thrashed around in the car, punctuating his cries with calls for help. Since we were almost at the mission, Ray told me to keep on driving. In his frenzy, the boy banged his arm on the car frame so hard that he broke it. Ray had all he could do to keep him from jumping out of the car or injuring himself further.

People all along the road turned to stare at the spectacle of the howling boy. As we entered the mission yard, several followed to see what was going on. One man came out ready to take us to court for so badly mistreating the child.

We took him back to the leprosy hospital, where his arm was put in a cast, and two days later we set out for Menz once again. This time the Cannatas were with us. Sam gave the boy two kinds of sedatives to calm him down on the trip. As before, he was friendly and talkative.

We were driving back on the same road we had come on two days earlier, and soon we neared the bridge over the creek. As it came into view, the boy began to howl and quiver like before. Due to the sedatives, he wasn't quite as wild, but he was definitely very agitated. This time we could understand what he was saying. Over and over, he repeated, "They're in the water. They're going to get me. They're trying to get on my back." As we crossed the bridge, he tried to jump out of the car.

The whole time this was going on, Sam kept talking to him about God's love and power, assuring him that he was safe with Jesus' protection. This definitely had a calming effect on him, and as we drove out of sight of the creek, he settled down again.

Our plane trip was without incident, and since he didn't live far from us, we offered to drive him home after we got back to our car. We had to cross two streams enroute, and he didn't react at all to either one of them. We delivered him safe and sound to his family.

We were eager for a chance to talk with our new Christian brothers, who understood such things. When we told them the story and identified the boy, they agreed that it was a case of demon possession. They said that children from "bad" or "evil" families are often susceptible to possession. Demons are believed to dwell in water, and Menz people have observed that if you fall asleep near water or are drunk there, you may become inhabited. Our friends were able to cite a number of cases of this type.

In December, just six months after the Mehal Meda meeting, we had another big gathering. This time we used the newly completed community hall in Tsahai Sina, near our house. We decided on a four-day meeting. Learning from previous experience with serving meat, we stuck to bread, tea, and fruit for those who came long distances. Negussie Tefera returned to Menz, and his messages were again timely and to the point.

The informal discussions in the evening were the highlight of each day. Those who had just been accepted back into their churches testified how the Lord had been with them in the midst of persecution. There were many evidences of the Lord's working in their lives.

The third night, everyone was awakened in the middle of the night by a deacon talking in his sleep. When they shone a flashlight on him, they found him pacing the floor with a haunted look in his eyes, mumbling unintelligibly. They tried to talk to him to get him to be quiet, but they had no success. He continued to move around and talk for the rest of the night.

When everyone woke the next morning, Negussie led in prayer. At the mention of Jesus' name, the young man who had been talking all night started screaming and fell on the floor in convulsions. Negussie immediately went to his side and began praying for him. Others added their prayers, claiming victory in Jesus' name over the forces at work in him. As we prayed, we witnessed something strange. In a deep voice, not at all resembling his own, he evasively answered Negussie's questions. When asked if a demon was controlling him, he answered, "Yes." First, he said he had seven, then forty, and finally eighty-seven demons.

When the demons were commanded to leave, the deep voice replied that it had permission to stay. "He's mine. I've lived here for years," we heard the eerie voice say. People drifted into the meeting and saw the convulsive, groaning boy on the hay. Their curiosity kept them from leaving.

We soon found out that the tormented boy came from Tigre, an area far north of Menz. He had chosen to come to Tsahai Sina because it has a well-known deacon training school. Young men usually leave home if they want to study full-time.

Our friends told us that casting out demons is very rare. Those in Menz know that *tenkways* and *wofas* (the witchdoctors who practice black magic) are the ones who invoke demons in the first place. Thus, it is left up to them to get rid of them if it becomes necessary. It is even generally believed that if the church tries to do anything about demon possession, the victim will die.

A majority of those watching recognized that what was happening was a battle between the power of God and that of Satan. The people who had experienced God's power added their fervent prayers to those already being offered. Because the young man had no relatives in the area, no one felt any specific responsibility toward him, and no one objected to our praying for him.

In Menz, it usually isn't possible to find a private place to pray since whole families live in a single room. They have no closet they can enter. But they have discovered a way to create privacy. When praying, they kneel on the ground and bend over until their forehead touches the floor. In this prone position, they cover their heads with the big shawl they always wear, and in this way, they are able to shut out the world. That morning the floor was covered with prostrate forms, each person claiming the power of Christ's sacrificial blood over the power of Satan.

We were aware of the possibility of the demons leaving him only to return sevenfold or to enter somebody else. So, we took everyone outside for a time of self-examination. We wanted to be clean vessels so that God could use us. The Bible teaches the value of the prayer of a righteous man. By receiving God's forgiveness and cleansing, we would be righteous.

We divided up into small prayer groups. Some confessed sins, some came to know Christ as Savior for the first time, and others just listened. After an hour of prayer and discussion, we reentered the hall. The battle was still going strong. As we again knelt to pray, we heard the demonic voice say that it had permission to stay until 1:00 p.m. Then the voice suggested that we cast the demons out in the name of Saint Mary or Saint George. It never mentioned the name of Jesus.

Due to the intensity of the warfare, we were unaware of the passing of time. When we did look at our watches, we were surprised to find that it was already one o'clock. All morning the young man had been unable to complete a single coherent remark. But as the appointed hour passed, his seizures began to subside, and finally, in a steady voice, he was able to claim victory in Jesus' name. We knew how Elijah must have felt when he challenged the prophets of Baal and won.

When everyone became convinced that he was actually free, joy began to overflow. The remainder of the day was spent in thanksgiving and praise to God. They knew a lot of songs by this time, and the singing during the meeting was indescribably beautiful. Every single person sang with a full voice, and their combined voices made the rafters ring. It thrilled our hearts to be part of it.

That evening, as we settled down in the hay again, the Lord led the discussion in a new direction. One deacon asked us to pray for his mother, as he felt she was in bondage to Satan. Several covenanted to pray with him, and we offered up a prayer right then. Then another deacon mentioned one of his relatives and requested prayer. This was the first time any of them had admitted these problems existed right in their own homes. With the day's experience still fresh in their minds, they dared to claim God's power over Satan right where they lived.

We were really convinced that the boy who had harbored a demon for so long needed Jesus to come in, in its place. It was essential for him to have his own Bible. Negussie suggested that we give one to him. Since we had made all the others pass a test to get one, we hesitated. We felt that he ought to take a test too.

Everyone gathered around to watch the performance of one who had so recently been under Satan's control. The test is hard, and many fail the first few times. We prayed for the Lord to give him a clear mind. Wonderfully, he was able to find every book called for, and he also knew what went before and after each one. He passed with flying colors. It was hard to believe that he was the same person we had observed the day before.

We had been saying for a long time that God was more powerful than the devil, but our Menz friends figured that we didn't really understand Satan's power. They doubted that we really knew what we were talking about. Then God revealed His power in such a graphic way that they would never forget it. The Lord was victorious as He freed the young man from the bonds of Satan.

But the enemy didn't accept defeat easily. He wasn't about to relinquish what he had held for so long. Menz was his territory, and he intended to keep it that way.

Stumbling Blocks

But food does not bring us near to God; we are no worse if we do not eat, and no better if we do. Be careful, however, that the exercise of your rights does not become a stumbling block to the weak. For if someone with a weak conscience sees you, with all your knowledge, eating in an idol's temple, won't that person be emboldened to eat what is sacrificed to idols? So this weak brother or sister, for whom Christ died, is destroyed by your knowledge. When you sin against them in this way and wound their weak conscience, you sin against Christ. Therefore, if what I eat causes my brother or sister to fall into sin, I will never eat meat again, so that I will not cause them to fall.

1 Corinthians 8:8–13

Ray and I were standing by our tent visiting one day in Kaya when suddenly, we heard terrible screams coming from the rug room. Filled with fear, we hurried to investigate.

Through the doorway, we beheld a shocking scene. Aschallew, one of our rug students, was holding his *doola* over his head. Then he brought it down with a resounding *whack* on the cowering form on the floor. After he saw us, he stopped, but his eyes were still ablaze with anger. He turned and stalked out.

A closer look told us that the victim was Ayalay, his weaving partner. He was covered with welts and bruises, but fortunately nothing was broken. When we asked him what had brought on the beating, he explained tearfully that he had been trying out his new scissors. Somehow as he snipped in midair, Aschallew's new shirt got in the way, and he cut it. He assured us that he hadn't meant to do it.

It took a week for him to recover enough to return to weaving. Then he had to work beside Aschallew on the loom again. It was awkward for both of them, but as the days passed, things seemed to settle down. Ayalay was much more careful with his scissors after that. We wondered if Aschallew would ever learn to control his temper.

All over Menz, people recognize certain old and beautiful trees as the habitation of evil spirits. Called *adbar* trees, they are regarded with great reverence and awe. No one would dare show disrespect for the tree by climbing it, cutting it, playing under it, or working close to it. Since these trees are never cut, they are the oldest and biggest around.

At prescribed times of the year, everyone takes offerings to the *adbar* to secure its blessing. These offerings may be sacrificial animals, such as chickens, sheep, or goats, or food like butter or honey. Sometimes fabric is hung on the tree, or decorations of chicken feathers are put on it. Whatever is given, the intent is the same. It is to honor the power dwelling there in return for its favor.

Scandalous news reached us one day that one of our Bible students had not only dared to approach an *adbar* tree, but he had taken away an offering someone had left. He removed a pot of butter, a very expensive and precious commodity in Menz. What was worse, he had used it to soften his dry, cracked feet.

We were right on our first guess as to who the culprit was. It was Aschallew. When we talked to him about it, he sheepishly admitted doing it. At the time, it had seemed like a good idea to him, since he knew it was senseless to worship a tree. He regarded it as a waste of good butter. But he hadn't realized what a furor it would raise. He admitted that maybe it wasn't such a smart idea after all.

Hardly a month passed before another incident arose. This time two students were involved. Orthodox Christians fast frequently, and the diet at those times is pretty plain, consisting of only grain and a few vegetables. It can get very monotonous.

Again, in his newfound freedom from the law, Aschallew decided it wasn't necessary to follow the fasting rules any longer. In order to demonstrate his convictions, he killed a chicken on a fast day and invited his friend Girma, also a deacon, to share it with him. They could have eaten it in secret, and no one would have been the wiser. But Aschallew wanted to make a point. So, they ate the chicken where everyone could see.

The reaction was immediate. The people were up in arms. It was just as they had suspected. This new foreign Bible made people break the law. It was against God. If the result of this new teaching was to make you do such things, they wanted no part of it. They barred Aschallew and Girma and their friends from speaking at church.

These people had waited for six months to get back into their churches, and now, overnight, they had lost the privilege to witness there. No one wanted to hear the opinions of a lawbreaker. When Aschallew saw the results of his impetuous behavior, he was crestfallen. He wanted to tell everybody about his newfound faith. He felt like shouting it. But now he had ruined his chances of telling anybody at all—at least for a while.

Aschallew reminded us of Peter in so many ways. When he got an idea, he just had to try it out immediately. If he felt something was wrong, he was anxious to set it right as soon as possible. He was impatient, outspoken, and blunt. We prayed that the Lord would work in his life and temper him.

Then the issue of fasting came up for the whole group. We knew it wasn't a new problem. Paul had faced exactly the same thing with the early Christians. He told them that all meat was good and was given by God to eat. But if eating meat kept him from being able to witness to his brother, he would continue to obey the Jewish law. He was willing to go without meat for as long as he lived, if necessary.

We realized it was time for a Bible study on the law and grace. Until the time of their salvation, they had kept the law in the hopes of being good enough to get into heaven. Now they were free from all that. They realized they would never make it on their own merits. They were judged guilty already, but Jesus had paid the penalty. Because of God's love and grace, they weren't going to get what they deserved. They had been forgiven.

Did that mean that they no longer needed to keep the law? Every one of them wanted to share his faith with his friends and relatives. No one would listen if they flaunted the law. If they really cared about others, they would have to guard against being a stumbling block. By breaking the law, they could draw people's eyes from Jesus to themselves.

Paul had circumcised Timothy, a half-Jew, when he wanted to take him with him to witness to the Jews. It wasn't a necessary part of his salvation, as he had become a believer some time earlier. It was done so that he wouldn't be a stumbling block to the Jews, as one outside the law. Paul did it so Timothy could witness to those who were law-abiding Jews.

Similarly, we encouraged them to keep obeying the law, but for a brand-new reason. They knew by now that law-keeping wouldn't secure their salvation. Instead, they were to keep the law out of love for their brothers. At that point, fasting changed from being a burden to being an active expression of their love for Jesus and those around them.

Frequently during our years in Ethiopia, we examined our own position in regard to Orthodox food laws. Of course, at first, we knew only a little, but the longer we lived in Menz, the more we learned. To behave like good Orthodox Christians, we would need to go without meat or animal products such as milk, cheese, butter, and eggs every Wednesday and Friday and for forty days before Easter. Also, we would need to give up eating any form of pork entirely, such as ham, hot dogs, or bacon. Rabbit, duck, and goose were also forbidden.

It was easy to eat what they ate and fast when they fasted when we were in their homes. But in their desire to be hospitable, they frequently served us milk during fast times when they had a surplus. They knew we didn't have the same fasting rules as they did and that we didn't like their crude barley beer. It upset them when we refused their hospitality, so we drank what was offered, and we said a silent prayer to God to protect us from tuberculosis or other diseases.

As we learned more and more about their food laws, we tried very hard not to be the cause of any problems. We were especially careful when they had tea at our house or ate a meal with us. Occasionally we slipped up and set out something that we shouldn't have. As soon as they recognized it and let us know, however, we quickly removed the offending food.

The question we faced now was this: After six years of living in Menz, since we knew more of the law, should we start keeping it? We studied the issue in the light of the New Testament and Paul's teaching on law-keeping, and we eventually found an answer. When the Gentiles became Christians, they didn't have to be circumcised and become Jews. They were asked only to keep a few Jewish food laws so they could eat with the Jews. It was agreed that their salvation came through grace, and it was not necessary to add the burden of the law.

That was a lot like the position we were in. We were not Orthodox. We had attained our salvation by grace before we ever became acquainted with the Orthodox laws. To add the laws later would imply a false admission that it is really keeping the law, after all, that saves.

We tried hard to be sensitive to the issue and were never made aware of any situation in which our eating habits served as a stumbling block. It is interesting to note that Menz people believe that the reason foreigners don't have demons is because we eat pork. They realized we were different in some way, but they didn't correctly identify the cause.

The new believers were forced to look carefully at some of their church practices too. Each spring there is a big celebration when the *Tabot* is taken out and paraded around in a formal procession. After the ceremonies, an ox is killed, and they feast on the raw meat.

We were invited to attend one of these holiday festivals, and as usual, we carefully observed all that went on. Before the ceremony, there was considerable bickering until all the people had paid a share of the price of the animal. When that was accomplished, it was slaughtered by a priest, as prescribed by law. He performed the task while holding his cross and adorned in his beautiful holiday priestly robe.

When we asked the purpose for killing the animal, we learned that here again was a sacrifice to Satan. They would offer him an ox in return for his leaving them alone for the coming year. They were trying to ensure against bad weather, sickness, accidents, infertility, lack of rain, and everything else attributed to the devil.

This was the first time our friends had come up against this practice since coming to know Jesus. They realized that they couldn't participate. Meat of this sort was a rare treat, but they refused to give any sort of honor to Satan. They knew that Jesus had already defeated him on the cross and that all they had to do was claim victory in Jesus' name.

They also began to think about idol worship. It was easy to see that worshiping the *adbar* tree was wrong. But as they seriously looked at their church, they recognized that some things in it had been made into idols as well.

Every Sunday morning, a priest would go around at the end of mass with either a cross or a Bible and bless each person. Few know what is inside the Bible or what the cross symbolizes, but all are most anxious to receive the blessing conferred by the holy object. Kissing the door of the church before entering, the floor inside, or the Bible afterward is not bad in itself. But for many, the very act is an attempt to make an invisible God into something they can see and worship and from which they can receive blessings.

Our friends had learned to worship God in spirit. Having all the right clothes and paraphernalia in a special holy place was no longer essential for them to worship God. They realized that He cannot be contained in a building, but He is present everywhere. That means they could pray to Him at any time, in any place.

In their new freedom, they didn't stop attending church. It is a good place to worship God, and they continued to perform their religious duties. But they began thinking about all they said and did, rather than just performing out of habit. They did the Bible reading in Amharic, rather than *Ge'ez*, during the service. They looked for, and found, new meaning in much of their church life.

The Increase

Then the church throughout Judea, Galilee and Samaria enjoyed a time of peace and was strengthened. Living in the fear of the Lord and encouraged by the Holy Spirit, it increased in numbers.

Acts 9:31

At the beginning of 1975, our rug class graduated in Kaya, and we took down our tents and moved back home. Each rug weaver set up his loom in his own home and began weaving independently, just like the weavers who had learned in the handcraft school in Tsahai Sina. We no longer saw them every day, but they still wanted us to come for Bible study.

So, we began TEE: Theological Education by Extension. The textbooks are written in Amharic and contain a short lesson for each day of the week, followed by questions that are to be answered as homework. Every Wednesday we met with them, and they were given a short, written quiz on the week's lessons. Then we had a time of review as they went over the answers to their homework. Most of the time, however, was spent discussing the application of the lesson to their everyday lives.

Lauralee Teaching TEE

There were always takers for anything free, so right from the start we asked each student to pay a deposit of one *birr* (dollar) for his book. They wrote all their answers in a separate notebook. At the end of the course, when they turned in their book, they got their money back.

Thirteen deacons enrolled in the first course and came regularly in Kaya. We met at Priest Girma's home although he was away in Addis at Priest School. He had two buildings on his compound, and his family only used one while he was gone. His wife was glad to let us meet in the other.

The first book studied was on prayer. As they learned what the Bible teaches about prayer, they began to think it over. Each lesson closed with a time of prayer. Many learned to pray for the first time in those classes.

There were some from Tsahai Sina who wanted to attend too, so they rode down with us every Wednesday. After two months, they asked us if we would start a similar class nearer home. They were sure a number of their friends would come. We agreed to give it a try.

They were right. There was an interest in TEE in Tsahai Sina too. Twenty-four signed up, and six of these were priests. The discussions with this group were livelier and more challenging than those in Kaya because of the presence of more priests and older students. Secure in their positions, they weren't afraid to challenge things and explore new ideas.

In April we started the second course in Kaya. This time nineteen enrolled, including one priest. We used two books—one on witnessing and the other on the gospel of John. After class one day, two young men stayed to ask if they could learn to preach like Muko and Negussie and the missionaries.

It was a good idea, and the time was right. We decided to have two student preachers a week in addition to the lesson. We would provide them with Scripture references and ideas as needed. After each class, we would talk to them privately, compliment them on their good points, and help them in any areas where they were weak.

Tatuk and Girma were the two who had come to us with the idea, so we asked them to be the first to try. Tatuk was a quiet young man of few words, but he was an excellent student of the Bible. Girma was both friend and pupil of Priest Girma. In Priest Girma's absence, the others looked to Girma as their spokesman. He was nearly a head taller than everyone else. This, coupled with his good looks and quick mind, combined to make him a natural leader.

Both were nervous the next week as they awaited their turn to stand in front of their fellow students. Their voices were shaky and weak as they began, but as they got involved in their subject, they lost some of their self-consciousness. They were very anxious to get their message across.

As we listened, we were as proud of them as if they had been our own children. We would have been pleased with whatever they did, of course. But our hearts were stirred by each in turn as they took a text from the Bible, explained it, and then applied it to their daily lives.

They didn't have either the Bible knowledge or the training in public speaking that we had, but as they talked, we became aware of something wonderful. They spoke Amharic without a single grammatical error. They never hesitated, seeking an elusive word or trying to think of the right verb form. They used graphic and picturesque words in just the right places. It was beautiful to hear. Also, they knew the exact problems their listeners were facing, and so the examples they gave were right to the point. Their very first sermons were better than the best we would ever deliver.

In succeeding weeks, everyone got a chance to preach, and as they practiced, their confidence grew. Soon some of them began preaching at their churches on Sunday mornings. Those from Akafee were the boldest, and Tatuk and Girma quickly became regular preachers.

Right along with all our Bible teaching, we kept on with community development projects. One thing that really concerned us was their farming methods. Some things, such as poor soil, harsh climate, lack of rain, and constant wind, can't be changed. These factors combine to make farming extremely difficult in Menz. But there were some things that could be improved.

Nearly every Menz field is covered with rocks—some of them quite large. In centuries past, slaves cleared the fields. But since slavery was abolished, no one does it anymore. They simply plow around the rocks and sow thinly in case it doesn't come up. They can't run the risk of losing all their seed. As a result, their crops are always very sparse.

We suggested clearing all the rocks from one field as a trial project. Abbee, a young father and deacon, said he was willing to give it a try. Working with him and another of our weavers, we spent two whole days in his field. Abbee's two small children came out and worked right along with us. Wheelbarrows break easily on rocky terrain and aren't something they could ever afford, so we carried the rocks on pieces of tin roofing nailed to poles, like a stretcher. It was backbreaking work, and progress was very slow, but finally we finished.

Children Clearing Rocks from Field

Ray suggested to Abbee that he plant twice as much grain as usual. Trustingly he did so. When his crop came up, it was truly beautiful. It was the best anywhere, and since he lived right beside the road, everyone passed by and saw it sooner or later.

When Priest Girma went to Addis to Priest School for a year, one of his greatest concerns was leaving his wife and children alone for such a long time. The only thing that reassured him was that the entire group of believers pledged to help his family whenever it was needed. They were true to their word. When it was planting time, they took Priest Girma's oxen and plow, prepared his land, and sowed his seed. With a lot of hands, the work went fast.

One day Ray and I went out and helped stack hay that the group had cut earlier in the week. With Priest Girma's wife as teacher, we learned the art of making beautiful stacks that don't tumble down or blow away in the wind. Another day we went with all the Bible students and helped her pick peas. The whole plant is pulled up and used, rather than just the peas. While we were out, a man on horseback came by and spotted us stooping in the sun. He couldn't believe his eyes. Foreigners out working in the field! He asked those nearest how much she paid us. We chuckled over that for a long time.

After clearing the field, they tied the plants up in huge bundles on cow hides and balanced them on their heads the mile back to the house. I carried little Yonas and everyone's jackets. After unloading everything, we all sat down in the dark coolness of her home, relaxing and talking together. There was lots of love and laughter in that room as we shared a simple meal.

A few weeks later, she came to us with a problem. All the hay Priest Girma had gathered the previous year to feed the oxen was used up. She had asked around the neighborhood, and nobody would sell her any.

In Menz, if you don't farm your inherited land every single year, it reverts back to the original family. Priest Girma's mother lived in the adjoining compound and was secretly hoping her son's wife wouldn't be able to farm the land. Then she could take it back again. To implement her plan, she went from door to door to all her neighbors and threatened them if they gave any help to Priest Girma's wife.

It didn't take the believers long to come up with a solution, once they heard the story. They knew someone who would sell hay. He lived a few miles away, but that wasn't a big problem. They took up a collection to pay for the hay, and they picked a day to haul it.

With our car and trailer, we went to meet them. We could only go as far as the cliff edge by the river valley. They carried load after load of hay up the steep hillside to our Land Rover parked at the top. We had good fellowship as everyone worked together to haul the hay and again when the hay was piled high in her yard. The crisis was averted. Her animals would be fed.

Deacon Taye, also a Bible student, had a very similar experience. He returned home from the fields one day to find his wife and children gone. Some of his chickens had been slaughtered, and their blood and feathers were splattered all over his house and yard. Grain had been stolen, and his house had been stoned. He was most unhappy.

We prayed with him for the Lord's intervention in the matter. He said his relatives were hoping to discourage him so that he would give up his inheritance and leave Kaya. But the Lord gave him patience, and a week later his wife returned. After that, the relatives gave up their attempts to get rid of him.

As problems came up in their lives, the new believers found that the Lord was sufficient. Each week they shared answers to prayer and told how the Lord was working in their lives. As the others heard their testimonies, they were strengthened.

One day we had a work party on the airstrip. We painstakingly hoed all the weed clumps on it with the help of a volunteer crew of rug weavers. We got lots of blisters, but we had fun working together, and it was worth it to have the strip in use again. Unfortunately, it didn't last long.

A few weeks later, the airstrip was closed again, this time by the government. Because of rebel uprisings, the new government wanted to be able to closely control all traffic in and out of Menz. Our strip was considered too isolated.

But we still had the road. When we first moved to Menz, it was unpaved over half the way from Addis. There were several months of the year when parts of it were impassable. Gradually it had been improved until there was an all-weather road all the way to Mehal Meda, where the Cannatas lived. That meant that we could drive in and out of Menz any time of the year, no matter how wet it was.

The last section of the road from Mehal Meda to our house was still just a dirt track, though, and a little rain made it treacherous. When it got good and muddy, it was hopeless. After our first rainy season there, when at least seventeen people drowned trying to cross the river on that stretch of the road, we built a bridge. That meant we could always get out of Tsahai Sina, at least on foot. We were never again trapped on our side of the river due to rain.

At Easter break time, our children flew up for a week's vacation. Since our Tsahai Sina strip was still closed, we drove to Mehal Meda to get them. We left early to meet the plane, as it took us longer to drive to the airstrip than it did for the forty-five-minute plane flight from Addis.

As we came in sight of the bridge, we sensed trouble. There was a crowd gathered around it, and smoke was billowing in the air. When we got closer, we saw the planking of the bridge, which we had worked so hard to build, was smoldering in a number of places. People on their way to the market had formed a bucket brigade from the river thirty feet below. They were using water pots, leather pouches, hats, and whatever else was handy to carry water to put out the fire.

It was obvious to us that their efforts were futile. Too much damage had already been done. A closer look showed that oil had been poured on the boards, and they had apparently been burning much of the night. There was no use in trying to stop it now. We still had a plane to meet, so we thanked them for their help, telling them they could go on to the market. Then we forded the river in our Land Rover and climbed the steep bank on the other side, glad once again that we had a four-wheel-drive vehicle.

Our children arrived right on schedule. We piled them and their belongings in our car and headed back home. When we dropped down into the river valley, we found a large army truck parked in the middle of the road. Soldiers with machine guns encircled it. They were facing outward, looking intently for any sign of the rebels who had challenged them to battle by burning the bridge.

We pulled up behind them, and they immediately ordered us to turn around and go back. At just that moment the machine-gun fire began. We didn't need to be asked twice. To the staccato accompaniment of machine-gun fire, we hastily retreated back up the hill and out of the valley. We could have returned to Mehal Meda right then, but our children were anxious to go home after having been away for several months.

Once before we had been on an old, unused back road parallel to the river. With the help of a few farmers along the way, we were able to follow the faint path once more, crossing the river close to home. The bridge was six miles from our house, and the action didn't come any closer that week. We were very thankful.

News reached us the day after the bridge burning that the daily bus out of Menz had been attacked in the Gwasa, an isolated grazing area, about half an hour after beginning its long trip to Addis. Rebels had succeeded in blocking the road in the same place twice before. Those times the bus just turned around and went back. But this morning they weren't so fortunate.

There were men waiting in ambush. They stopped the bus at gunpoint, murdering the driver and a policeman, and critically injuring several others. The passengers were then robbed and left to flee in terror to safety as best they could. Sam had to sew up several of the more seriously injured victims that afternoon. After that episode, the bus company quite understandably shut down service to Menz.

Rebels also cut the telephone lines to the single phone in Mehal Meda and felled some of the poles. Harassment continued in every corner of Menz, and the government troops were kept running from one spot to another. Their retaliation was swift and effective. They burned the homes and crops of everyone suspected of harboring rebels or any other form of disloyalty.

With conditions so unsettled everywhere in Menz, the new believers were no longer singled out for persecution. They had a time of peace. People had too many other things to worry about to be concerned with them. They were finally free to study and grow—and they did.

The Outcastes

Then Peter began to speak: "I now realize how true it is that God does not show favoritism but accepts from every nation the one who fears him and does what is right."

Acts 10:34–35

We still thought sometimes about Wuhay. Our first efforts to teach there had resulted only in a ripped tent. Since that time, some deacons and a priest from there had become fairly regular Bible students. They begged us to give Wuhay a second chance.

Awlachew was particularly insistent, and so we finally agreed. He made arrangements for us to visit his church on the next big holiday. When we arrived that day, the people greeted us warmly and even invited us inside the church for mass. Afterward they asked Ray to preach in the courtyard. As usual, he took advantage of the occasion to tell them about Jesus.

After the preaching, they divided into groups in numerous small huts scattered around the church yard. Each group is named for a saint and selects its own members, something like a fraternity. Those who aren't chosen by any group stay outside. Within, there is an abundance of bread and *tella* that the members have provided. After a series of special rituals and blessings, they begin eating and visiting. If there is any food left over, they give it to the poor waiting outside.

Before we left that day, the church leaders came to us and asked if we would come and teach rug weaving or some other craft in Wuhay. They were finally receptive. We promised to consider it and told them we'd return for the next holiday.

Several months earlier, one afternoon as we were driving to our house, our attention was attracted by a young man at the side of the road. He was waving at us to stop. We had noticed him at several places in the last few months, and his face had become familiar. His right leg was withered to a useless stump below the knee, and he walked on his left leg with the aid of a cane.

He told us his name was Wolde Tsadik and asked if we could teach him some type of craft. He had already gone to school as far as the sixth grade, but to go any further, he would have to leave home. His family just couldn't afford to send him to Mehal Meda to live. Because of his handicap, he was unable to be of much help to them.

Ray was teaching rug weaving at the time, but a weaver has to stand all day, using both hands. Rug weaving was out of the question for Wolde Tsadik. We weren't able to help him with any craft right then, but we did invite him to attend the Tsahai Sina TEE classes and Sunday Bible studies.

Wolde Tsadik came faithfully to every class we held in that area. Because he had been to school, he could read, and he learned quickly. In spite of his handicap, he always had a ready smile, and he soon made many friends. He was a frequent passenger when we went to teach in Kaya, and he easily became an accepted member of the group there. Before long he became a born-again believer.

One afternoon he stayed after class to talk to us. He began by telling us a very unusual story. A few months earlier, a horse had died in his neighborhood. After it happened, the neighbors got together and held a council. They ruled that it was the fault of Wolde Tsadik's family. His family was ordered to pay twenty-three dollars for the dead animal.

They had no choice but to pay what was demanded, so they went about the task of getting the money together. Since they didn't have that much cash on hand, they had to sell some things as well as borrow from relatives. It really caused them a hardship. They finally got enough money and paid it to the owner of the horse. A week later, the man's small child died. Grief-stricken, he brought the twenty-three dollars back and flung it at them. He told them they could keep the money if they would just leave him and his family alone and not bother them again.

The story made no sense to us. It just didn't add up. It was obvious there was something we didn't understand, so we asked him to tell it to us again. Had he or his family touched the animal or fed it anything? He denied it. And so, as often happened, we gave up, not really understanding. It just reminded us once again that we were foreigners in their culture.

After finishing his story, Wolde Tsadik had a request to make. We had been teaching that God was more powerful than Satan. For the past few weeks, his mother had been having spells and convulsions. He felt that she was being troubled by the devil. Would we come and pray for her?

He told us he lived across the river at Wuhay. We already had a date to go back to the church there the next Tuesday. We could combine the two visits. We agreed to come and committed the matter to the Lord. We didn't know what awaited us at either place, and so our only resource was prayer. We did a lot of it that week.

We asked Muko to go along with us for the day. A large crowd had gathered outside the church, and mass was already in progress when we arrived. As we entered the courtyard, no one welcomed us or invited us to participate, so we sat down and waited. Finally, the mass was over, and everyone came out of the church. An old priest then read an especially long passage from "Miracles of Saint Michael" in *Ge'ez*. We were ignored as completely as if we were invisible.

Next, they went to their small huts to eat, and at that time we were urged to join one of the groups. Since we made the effort to follow their customs whenever it was at all possible, we didn't refuse. Inside the hut, one of the men knelt on the ground on all fours with a stack of bread on his back. As he knelt, a priest spoke some words over him.

Then they ate and talked. As we tried to understand everything going on around us, all three of us had the same impression. There was nothing in that room or ceremony that honored God. We felt we couldn't stay there any longer. Saying hasty goodbyes, we returned to our car and drove off. No one tried to detain us. Once again God had closed the door to our beginning work in Wuhay.

Wolde Tsadik's house was about two miles away. He was waiting for us by the road when we arrived. Loping along in front of the car, he guided us to his house close by. As we parked in front of his compound, we beheld a strange sight. There were broken pot shards all over the yard. It was obvious that his relatives were pottery makers. As far as we knew, only outcastes made pottery. Just to make sure, we asked Muko. He knew a little more about the customs than we did, and he had drawn the same conclusion. Our friends must be outcastes.

Outcastes. The very word felt strange on our tongues. It is a concept we associate with Bible times, not with the twenty-first century. But when we moved to Menz, we learned that outcastes still exist today and are just as unpopular and feared as ever.

Every five or ten miles in Menz, there is a compound of pottery workers. They acquire their status at birth by being born to outcaste parents, and there is no way they can change it. They must always marry others in their same class, so the class system is perpetuated generation after generation.

Outcastes aren't allowed to own farmland, but they are permitted to farm on the cliffsides, where no one else wants to make the effort to work. Because they can't depend on farming, they are forced to work with their hands for a living. As craftsmen, they are the only ironmongers or metalworkers in Menz. They fix the plows and scythes that every farmer uses in his work. They first make the tools and then sharpen them as needed.

They also make pottery, and because of this, they are sometimes called pottery workers in derision. Being very skilled in this art, however, they make a wide array of clay utensils. Because they are dependent on what people are willing to pay for their wares, they must work very hard to make a living.

No one else in Menz would consider doing either metal or pottery work. Even selling such an object at the market brands you as one of them. Outcastes also weave cloth and do some other types of handwork, but these are crafts that are common to the rest of the people. They are considered second-class citizens at church. They can never advance to the level of a deacon or priest or become any type of religious leader. They are merely tolerated as fringe participants in the church activities.

There are outcastes in other parts of Ethiopia who claim Jewish ancestry. They are still quite strict in their observance of Old Testament Jewish laws. In Menz, they seem to have forgotten this heritage altogether, especially the younger generation. Yet some of them still return to the old settlements when they become aged and remain there until they die.

By far, the worst part of being an outcaste is that people believe they have a *budda*, or evil eye. The rest of the population lives in fear and trembling of these cursed people and the harm they are thought to perpetuate. Fear is greatest when it's dark, especially in the hours just before dawn. Many are convinced that outcastes turn into jackals and rob graves at night, and most believe they can bring a curse on you that will cause sickness or even death.

As a result, on community market days, outcastes are compelled to sit in a separate place to sell their pottery and metalwork. People avert their eyes and step aside to avoid them when they pass on the road. Eating with or sleeping in the same room as an outcaste is considered out of the question.

All little children in Menz have a special type of haircut. Their heads are shaved except for a single clump of fluffy hair left in front. The parents hope that this will distract the *budda* so he won't look the child in the eye and curse him. They also make sure the child wears a string of charms against this dreaded possibility.

All this flashed through our minds when we saw the pottery shards outside the house. We also recalled the story of the dead horse. At last, it made sense. The people thought Wolde Tsadik's family had killed it with an evil eye.

We had known from the start that there were outcastes in Menz, but they made up only about 3 percent of the population. We intended to work with them after we'd had some success with the Orthodox majority. We had met a few outcastes and knew that they were very nice people, but that was as far as we had gotten.

We got out of the Land Rover, now doubly curious as to what we would find. Not only had Wolde Tsadik said the devil was troubling his mother and that she might have a demon, but they were outcastes. The family welcomed us warmly, however, urging us to come inside. The house was swept and clean, and they all had on their best clothes. Instead of busying themselves fixing us something to eat and drink, as Menz hosts invariably do, they asked us to sit down with them and talk.

Wolde Tsadik's mother had something she was very anxious to say. She told us that she had become aware of some unusual things ever since her son had been going to Bible classes. Each time he heard a lesson or a sermon, he came straight home and passed on all that he had learned. They were all glad for a chance to learn too.

His mother explained that she was in the habit of boiling a special little pot of coffee when she wanted to know if she should do a certain thing—such as go on a trip or visit a friend. Both the pot and the brightly colored cloth that went with it had come from the *tenkway*. By performing certain rituals with the stirring stick and observing the smoke, she would receive her answer. But lately, things had been going wrong. Every time she began doing this, she had convulsions and fell down, rolling on the floor.

As she thought about her problem in relation to Wolde Tsadik's teaching, she became convicted that what she was doing was wrong. She was honoring Satan instead of God. She had some other charms, too, and as she told us her story, she brought out all the paraphernalia she had gotten from the *tenkway* and laid it at our feet. "Burn all of this," she said. "I never want to see it again. I know it's wrong to have it. From now on I'm going to depend only on Jesus Christ."

We were stunned. This was a woman speaking. For five years I had taught women. When I asked them what they thought about anything, they would just giggle and reply, "Oh, we're too stupid. We don't know anything. We're only women."

I had become very frustrated trying to convince them they could learn. But it didn't do any good. They had never been to school for a single day. Nobody had ever asked them their opinion, except about household tasks, and they had been told over and over that they were stupid. It's no wonder that they believed it.

Yet here was a woman to whom God had spoken, and she had understood. She freely shared her feelings with us. Then we told her that the One she really needed to confess to was God. It was against Him that she had sinned, and He was the only One who could forgive her. She didn't need to be punished for her sins, for Jesus had already paid the price.

At this time, only a few priests and deacons in Menz could comfortably talk to God. The idea of a woman praying was an unheard-of concept. We decided that we would guide her prayer. We would say a line, and she could repeat it after us. It was too much to expect her to grasp the idea of prayer and then express her own thoughts as well.

We bowed our heads, and Muko prayed first. Then, as he was getting ready to lead her, she began to pray by herself. It was very simple and clear. "God, You know how all my life I've gone to the *tenkway* whenever there was sickness in the family or if I needed anything. Fear of Satan was a big thing in my life, and so I've done a lot of things to honor him. Now I realize that was all wrong, and I want to say I'm sorry. I never want to do that again. From now on, I'm only going to trust in Jesus. Amen." There was no doubt in our minds that she understood what prayer was, and we were sure the angels in heaven were rejoicing at that moment.

As soon as she finished, her oldest daughter started praying. She was a young woman whose husband had divorced her. On top of that, her only child had died. She, too, poured out her heart to God and asked Jesus to come into her life. Then the other daughter prayed. When Wolde

Tsadik's turn came, he could hardly contain his joy. His two brothers and sister-in-law were there also, and they listened carefully to everything that was said, but they didn't join in that day.

Before we left, they asked if we would come back and show filmstrips at their house sometime. We hesitated, secretly wondering if anyone would come. They read our thoughts and quickly allayed our doubts by saying, "We think our neighbors will all come. They are more interested in seeing cinemas than they are afraid of us. Besides, they don't think evenings are such a bad time to be with us."

So, we began showing filmstrips there. Wolde Tsadik and a friend went from house to house all over the area announcing our coming. We would arrive to find a packed house. They managed to squeeze seventy into their one-room dwelling. We really had "close" fellowship there. After the filmstrip, Wolde Tsadik preached a sermon. It was a good one. The people enjoyed it so much that they hated to leave when it was over. They made us promise to come back the next week.

When we went back to our class in Kaya a couple of days later, we told them the whole story, only omitting Wolde Tsadik's name. They were as excited and incredulous as we had been. At the end, we told them the young man involved was a friend of theirs. They immediately began guessing who it might be. Finally, we had to tell them. They found it very hard to believe. Wolde Tsadik was such a nice guy. They had never before realized an outcaste could be such a good friend. They really thought a lot of him. It was plain to see they couldn't quit liking him at that point. So, God showed them that He loves everyone, and He gave each of them some of that same love for Wolde Tsadik.

As outcastes, Wolde Tsadik's family had suffered persecution all their lives. Wolde Tsadik knew of the trials that those accused of eating donkey meat had gone through. Yet he could see that in spite of it all, they still had the joy of the Lord in their lives. He asked if some of them would come and share their faith and pray with his family. Tatuk and Girma accepted gladly. We took them to Wuhay, and as they sat and shared experiences and prayed together, there was an almost-tangible bond of oneness. The next time we showed filmstrips there, Girma went along and preached afterward.

We had prayed for an open door in Wuhay, but God hadn't opened the one we expected. Instead, He had surprised us and opened a trapdoor. As we looked back, we were so thankful that we were in the right place at the right time to fall through it. God not only established a witness in Wuhay, but at the same time He began to break down a barrier that had stood unchallenged for centuries.

Growing Stronger

As they traveled from town to town, they delivered the decisions reached by the apostles and elders in Jerusalem for the people to obey. So the churches were strengthened in the faith and grew daily in numbers.

Acts 16:4–5

Six months had passed since our last revival meeting. It was time to have another one. It had been exactly a year since our big meeting in Mehal Meda and a lot had happened in that time. In May 1975, we invited John Cheyne and Negussie back, as well as one of our new missionaries, Jimmy Maroney.

A week before the meeting, we heard that Negussie would not be able to come. We were disappointed, but we could still go on, using Muko as a preacher and translator. Then we got word on the radio that Jimmy Maroney was in the hospital with a serious infection. That left only John. The day before our meeting he came down with a high fever. As is frequently the case in Africa, he had malaria. Medicine would cure him, but not in time for our meeting. It was too late to cancel the meeting and get word out to everyone, so we decided to go ahead without any visiting preachers. With Muko's help, we would just do the best we could.

Muko grew up in Southern Ethiopia, in the area of Wollamo. The Christian church there grew miraculously when all the missionaries were expelled during the period of the Italian invasion from 1936 to 1941. That amazing story is well told in the book *Fire on the Mountain* by Raymond Davis.

Muko went to public school as far as the tenth grade. He was an excellent student and was very active in his church. With the help of some SIM (Sudan Interior Mission) missionaries, he went to dressers school, where he trained to be an advanced male nurse. After graduation he worked in one of their hospitals until Sam found him.

We were just beginning mission work in Menz. Sam wanted an Ethiopian helper to go with him on his mobile clinics as well as to work in the Tsahai Sina clinic. It was there that Sam stored his medical supplies and held clinic every Thursday morning. He needed someone to provide medical care there all the time.

Muko was both intrigued with the idea of going to Menz and afraid of the place as it had such a bad reputation. But he felt the Lord's leading, so he agreed to give it a try. He moved into a room of the clinic right after we finished building our house nearby. We got acquainted with Menz together.

Amharic was a second language for Muko, just like it was for us, and he came to Menz at the same time as we did. But he asked lots of questions and was a keen observer. It wasn't long before we began depending on him to help us understand what was going on around us and what was being said. We also discovered he had a terrific sense of humor. As a mimic he was unbeatable. We were sure to have fun when Muko was around.

His medical practice started small. At first his patients came with fear and trembling, and only as a last resort. But he had a reassuring manner, and they found help coupled with a genuine concern for their health. They began telling their friends and neighbors, and soon he had so many patients that his days started at sunup and often continued long past nightfall. If a person was too sick to be moved, Muko made house calls—on a mule if one was provided; on foot if not.

Sometimes emergencies came in the middle of the night. Wailing relatives would come begging for help. Muko found it hard to refuse anybody, so he usually went with them. Although Muko's training was limited, he met up with a wide range of ailments every day. What he didn't know, he looked up in his medical books, asked Dr. Cannata, or simply depended on the Lord for direction. His natural talent, combined with God's help, made him into an exceptionally good doctor in a few short years. It wasn't long before everybody knew and loved him.

Sam made a practice of beginning his clinics with a preaching service while the instruments were in a pot on the Bunsen burner being sterilized. He often asked Muko to preach. Muko wasn't content until he was able to catch the interest of the most unconcerned patient. He soon grew to be as good a preacher as he was a doctor.

We knew how busy Muko was at the clinic. Nevertheless, he agreed to help us in any way he could at the three-day meeting. He loved these gatherings as much as everyone else. Due to all the political unrest in Menz at the time, we didn't think it wise to have a public meeting in the community hall. It was time for a little discretion.

We were already having frequent Bible studies at our house and our living room–dining room area was fairly large. By moving out most of the furniture and seating people on the floor, we could squeeze in about sixty. It was a convenient meeting place because Muko could run back and forth to the clinic as needed. An added benefit was that we had running water available and lights at night.

When we began the meeting on Sunday afternoon, a group of government school students came from Mehal Meda. Our Orthodox Bible students were very self-conscious. They felt like country bumpkins next to the educated town students. They were afraid they would appear ignorant if they said anything, so they clammed up. We taught into the evening but didn't have the participation and feedback that we had come to expect.

The next morning all the students went back to school. Then the others began to participate. The greatest need at that meeting was for them to apply the Gospel to their everyday lives in Menz. Muko was the right preacher for the occasion. He had a knack for presenting things in such a graphic way that the conclusion was obvious. Yet when you grasped it, you felt as if you had just made a big discovery.

One of the major problem areas was that of sex. Premarital sex and adultery are the norm rather than the exception in Menz. Nights are frigid, and beds and blankets are scarce. Sleeping alone just isn't practical. A good host always provides for his guest's every need, including a girl to keep him warm.

Marriages in Menz are very shaky affairs. They are terminated frequently, often over trivial things. When women remarry, their children automatically become stepchildren and as such are usually treated very badly. By our observation, about a third of the children in Menz were illegitimate, and another third were stepchildren.

Accepting Jesus as Lord meant that these young men had to take a new look at everything in the light of God's standards. Muko challenged them to regard their bodies as temples of God, not to be spoiled in any way by what they ate, drank, or did. He had lived unmarried in Menz for five years without the common convenience of a *gared*, a live-in servant girl. It was possible to live to please God. He could tell them from personal experience. They listened to him because they knew what he said was true. He had lived in Menz long enough to be one of them.

Arekay is a very strong drink made in Menz. Its effects are visible everywhere in battered women, bruised children, and broken homes. It's even possible to get drunk on the local beer of *tella* if you drink enough of it. Many were convicted of the sin of drunkenness, and some who had serious drinking problems vowed never to drink again.

Then, too, we spent time discussing what they should do about sacrifices to the *borenticha* and the *adbar*. Methodically they examined their lives to see if anything remained that honored Satan.

At noon we divided them into small groups and asked each group to make up a short play about some problem area in Menz life, then show the Christian response to the problem. Menzies are born actors. They were full of ideas, and an hour later they were ready to perform. The house was packed as the first group faced the waiting audience. They depicted a family land feud, including the bribing of a judge. The next drama showed a young person leaving home and wasting all his family's money on women and drink.

Another team included a deacon dressed as an old woman who went to the *tenkway* for advice. With makeshift props, he went through all the elaborate rituals. The last two groups portrayed things concerning the church. All were convincingly true. They had captured the essence of Menz. Interestingly enough, no matter what the situation was, it always ended the same. Everyone grabbed their *doolas*, and a free-for-all began. It was somewhat perilous in our living room, but there was no doubt that the dramas were authentic.

Living Room Drama

After the dramas we turned the rest of the meeting over to them. They took turns giving testimonies of God's work in their lives and sharing spiritual insights. They spoke all afternoon and late into the night. Many new Bible students were there, and most were only in their late teens or early twenties. Since they were unmarried, they were still living at home. God convicted several of them of the need to accept Jesus as Savior. Rebelliousness and disobedience to parents were mentioned again and again as these young men told what was on their hearts.

When they came to a personal knowledge of Christ as Savior, they realized their Christianity was no longer based solely on their baptism. They broke the strings around their necks that had been the badge of their faith since they were babies. The transformation in their lives was proof enough.

Getacher, a shy boy of sixteen, haltingly told of his desire to have Jesus as Lord of his life. When he arrived home from the meeting the next day, he found his family sacrificing the *borenticha*. He had only been a believer for twenty-four hours, and he was already facing a test. Fully convinced of the wrongness of it, he refused to take part.

At first his family pleaded with him, then they threatened to throw him out if he didn't change his mind. But Getacher didn't budge. As a result, they made him leave home, and they went on with the ritual. Several weeks passed, and in his own quiet way he stayed close to Christ. Because of his patience and humility, they finally relented and let him return.

A number of the believers were teaching and preaching in various places. Abeje, a young deacon weighing only about seventy pounds, taught fifteen neighborhood children Bible stories twice a week. Asefa, the young man who had asked us to come to Kaya in the first place, had gotten the job he wanted and had moved to Zeret. It was about a three-hour walk beyond Kaya at the tip of the peninsula.

He taught Bible studies several times a week—sometimes to the students at the government school next door and sometimes to the priests and deacons from the local church. Every time he had to go to Mehal Meda to get his salary, he scheduled his trip to coincide with a meeting of the Kaya group. He had been sure that if they heard the Bible, they would believe it, and he was right. He wasn't surprised at all. It had happened just like he expected.

The rains started right on schedule in June. We began working seriously on rebuilding the burned bridge. When we originally built it, the mission did all the work and supplied all the materials with almost no help from the people. Now they had grown accustomed to using it. They were pretty upset when it was burned, and they wanted to help us rebuild. They brought eucalyptus trees from all over to be used as planking.

The trees were cut to length and hammered in position with a sledgehammer. Then they were covered with crushed rock. We made sure that the bridge wouldn't burn easily a second time. It was finished just before the heavy rains made the river impassable. We were proud of that rebuilt bridge. It hadn't cost us anything. What was more important, it was a project that had required community cooperation.

We stopped going anywhere for Bible studies when the road got good and muddy and settled down to enjoy the daily deluges. Our children flew home for summer vacation, and we were able to spend some wonderful time together as a family.

The rains also brought the fighting around us to a standstill. The government trucks full of soldiers couldn't travel on the slick roads. Foot travel was risky because rivers rose quickly, and if you weren't careful, you could be trapped on the wrong side. So, a truce went into effect for the duration of the rains.

The rains signaled that it was again time for the Rainy Season Bible School. All during the past year we had been in frequent contact with the Orthodox Mission in Addis. Their radio singer had made us some song tapes. Priest Mekebub, who also worked there, had originally come from Menz. He went with Sam a number of times and preached at clinics and Bible studies.

Every year *Ato* Gebre Hiwet had been the propelling force behind the Rainy Season Bible School. He found the teachers and then provided for their stay in Menz. But now he was in prison. People in Menz were discouraged. They were sure there wouldn't be any Bible school this year.

In our visits to the Orthodox Mission, we became the contact point between those in Menz who wanted another Bible school and the Orthodox leaders in Addis. We prayed for months that the Lord would work out the details if there was to be a school this year. We had seen before that those who got interested in the Bible at the Bible school were the ones who later followed through to complete trust in Christ.

Their former teacher, whom everyone had loved so much, had been transferred to Northern Ethiopia. It would be hard to find anyone to take his place, but the Lord led us to Isaias. Named for the Old Testament prophet, he lived up to his name. He knew his Bible well, having studied in a school where there was regular Bible instruction by BCMS (Bible Churchmen's Missionary Society). He was a frequent preacher on the Orthodox radio program, and he knew and loved Jesus. God had again answered our prayers far beyond our expectations.

During the first week of the Bible school, Jimmy Maroney taught a daily class on how to preach. A lot of students had become really interested in this subject. For the duration of the Bible school, two students a day preached to their classmates. For the first time, we attended a lot of the classes. Of course, we wanted to hear our students preach, but we also really enjoyed Isaias's Bible studies. He was able to make the Scriptures really live. He preached every Sunday at Tsahai Sina Maryam church and then taught our regular Bible class afterward.

Graduation day was like no other. The rain was pelting noisily on the tin roof as we gathered in the community hall. One hundred and twenty students were there, along with their relatives and friends. They began by singing some of the songs they had been practicing all month. Then came the best part. They acted out the story of the prodigal son. Its setting was present-day Menz, and it seemed perfectly natural. They were very convincing.

At that point some boys crawled out covered with brown wool blankets. They scrambled around on their hands and knees on the stage making strange barking noises. Then it dawned on us. They were supposed to be pigs! No one in Menz had ever seen the forbidden animals, so they had used their imaginations. The result was both unique and hilarious, and the play was a great success.

We made many new friends at the Bible school, and as we had done each preceding year, we awarded prizes at graduation. To the ones who already had Bibles, we gave songbooks and concordances. Others chose pocket New Testaments.

The Bible school was only a month long instead of the usual six weeks, but we felt it was the best ever. There seemed no limit to God's working. Things were getting better all the time. We wondered what could possibly happen next. We didn't have to wait long to find out.

Protection

*One night the Lord spoke to Paul in a vision: "Do not be afraid;
keep on speaking, do not be silent. For I am with you, and no one
is going to attack and harm you, because I have many people in this city."
So Paul stayed in Corinth for a year and a half,
teaching them the word of God.*

Acts 18:9–11

We began to feel effects of the political changes in Ethiopia. Gas was rationed everywhere. Only four gallons a week per car were allowed with a rationing coupon at designated stations. We brought all our gas to Menz in large metal drums and kept our supply in the garage, siphoning it out as needed. Getting permission to buy whole drums of gas was almost impossible. We drove only when absolutely necessary.

Supplies at the market kept getting scarcer and scarcer. Salt and sugar became precious commodities to be hoarded. Flour was often unavailable. Kerosene and diesel—the fuel for simple lanterns in Menz—could no longer be found. Black marketeers could name their price when they were able to produce the precious goods.

With telephone and bus lines frequently out of commission and wages far overdue, the *Baite Kahinet* of the Orthodox Church in Menz folded. With its collapse, the chance for Priest Girma to become an official Bible teacher for Menz disappeared. In September he graduated from Priest School—number one on the final exam out of 112 priests from all over Ethiopia. He returned to Menz to find that his opportunity had vanished.

As the rains slackened, the war in Menz escalated again. By this time, both airstrips were closed by the government. Right after our children went back to boarding school, the rebels blocked the road to Addis. They let it be known that any passing by would be shot. Ray and I were the only missionaries in Menz at the time, and we decided it was wisest to stay right where we were.

The government troops scoured the countryside, trying to find any trace of the elusive fugitives. They destroyed everything in their path. Dark, billowing clouds of smoke on the horizon from smoldering thatch roofs became a common sight.

As the people fled before the troops, they passed right by our house. They carried as much as possible with them, taking care not to laden themselves so heavily that they couldn't move quickly. They had to be able to outrun trucks. Many of them brought their belongings to us to store in the handcraft school. Ray carefully labeled each bundle or trunk and then stacked it inside. Before very many days passed, one large room was packed full, from floor to ceiling, as well as a smaller storeroom.

Priests from our neighboring church even brought the ark for us to store and guard, as well as some other holy books and relics in a wooden chest. Only six months earlier, we had been accused of stealing arks. Now we were being asked to guard one!

The rebel contingent was made up of local people united under the leadership of two brothers who had just had their huge dairy ranch and other landholdings nationalized. In defiance of the new government, they went to Menz to lead a resistance movement. The rebels looked no different from the rest of the people, and it was almost impossible to locate them. Yet it was obvious they were there since they kept striking out at the government.

Jets were brought in for the battle. First helicopters flew low, reconnoitering the countryside. People ducked for cover to escape their scrutiny when they heard the steady throb of their rotors. Next the jets descended, accompanied by an earsplitting scream. The people were terrified. They tried to hide, but they couldn't escape the noise. The jets flew over again and again, firing high-caliber incendiary cannon rounds into houses where the rebels were suspected to be hiding. The government troops moved in quickly in the wake of the strafing. Only the fleet of foot escaped.

From our house we had a ringside seat. We tried hard not to take sides, and both the government troops and the rebels were careful not to involve us in the conflict. We didn't feel at any time that either side resented our presence.

For those two months, our only link to the outside world was the shortwave-radio contact we had each morning. Everyone was very concerned about our safety and felt that our lives were in jeopardy because of the exaggerated rumors in Addis about the fighting. We tried hard to convey to them the assurance God had given us that He was in control.

We felt that we were exactly where he wanted us to be and that our protection was His responsibility. We had long believed that the safest place to be was in the center of God's will. Now we were getting a chance to test our convictions. We didn't leave our compound or hold any meetings during that time, but plenty of people came to see us. Many just wanted a chance to talk and receive some reassurance. We had an unlimited opportunity to share our faith.

The government school teachers and workers had left when the bus was attacked several months earlier, and they hadn't returned. We were almost the only outsiders left in Menz. As people came to see us, they expressed wonder that we would continue to stay in Menz when we didn't have to. We could have left months ago. They recognized that our staying was by choice, and they told us again and again how much they appreciated it. We were finally accepted as one of them as we stuck out the war together—something we hadn't accomplished by living there for seven years in peacetime.

LAURALEE LINDHOLM

The house burning continued day after day, but it was always some distance away. One day it looked as if our turn had come at last. Through the binoculars we could see new blazes moving steadily in our direction. We watched their approach all during the long afternoon. The smoke plumes got to within half a mile of us just as the sun went down. With a houseful of tearful people cowering behind us, we saw the troops come over the rise toward the house across the road.

All the women of the compound had fled to our house, and the men were out hiding in the fields. The soldiers ordered them to come out of hiding. Then they commanded the women to return home. They had done enough for the day and wanted a place to sleep and a hot meal. As a result, that compound escaped harm.

The next morning, they moved on to Kaya. As we watched the black clouds of smoke rise, we thought of our many friends there. We were much in prayer for them as we awaited news of what had happened. When we did hear the story, we were thrilled again to hear of God's unmistakable planning and His protection of His own.

After the troops got to Kaya, they went straight to Priest Girma's house. Many of them had met him when they were in training in Addis, next door to the Priest School. Several had come to know Jesus through him. He had invited them to visit him if they ever came to Menz. After talking for a while, they had left his home and went on with their business. Two men in Kaya were suspected of being leaders of the resistance movement. The soldiers went to those two compounds and burned them. Surprisingly, however, they didn't touch or harm anything else enroute, as they had in other places. So, Kaya was spared.

One of our Bible students lived in a compound adjoining that of a suspected rebel leader. When the troops appeared on the horizon, everyone fled but Gooltaye. He wanted to tell them not to burn his house. He had nothing to do with rebels or the war, and he thought they ought to know it. As they approached, he began explaining. Before he could finish his first sentence, however, one of the soldiers radioed headquarters on the shortwave strapped to his back. He transmitted his location and requested orders for the present operation.

Gooltaye stepped closer to hear better. There was no mistaking the sharp reply commanding them to destroy everything and everyone they found there. Gooltaye didn't wait for the rest of the conversation. He had heard enough. He fairly flew out of the compound and made a beeline for the nearest grass. The Lord saved Gooltaye that day, and as he recounted his narrow escape, he was sure it was for a purpose.

When the soldiers had burned houses the previous spring, many people immediately bought new grass and rethatched them before the rains. Now, only six months later, they were burned again. This time the people were in no rush to rebuild. There was no future in it. They would just have to live in them like they were, charred and roofless.

In October, after weeks of heavy fighting, we heard rumors that the troops had caught sight of the rebels and had boxed them in a canyon. With their helicopters and trucks of soldiers, they moved in on the tired and desperate men on foot. At last, their persistence paid off. They surrounded the rebels and, after much shooting, finally got a firsthand look at their elusive quarry.

The two rebel leaders were already dead. They had shot themselves rather than be taken alive. To settle all doubts about their deaths, their heads were taken back and displayed in the market in Mehal Meda and on television in Addis. They were proof that the now almost-legendary Biru brothers had at last been defeated.

The government troops retaliated for a few more weeks in areas with suspected rebel sympathizers, but the war had finally ended, at least for the time being. The road was reopened, and we were able to go to town. As we went, we praised God, not only for His protection during those difficult days, but also for the freedom from fear we had experienced.

We took Wolde Tsadik with us to the leprosy hospital in Addis. A missionary friend on the staff had said they could help him. After examining his leg, they recommended amputating it at the knee. Then they could make him an artificial leg. They estimated it would take about a month to heal, and then he could be fitted with a prosthesis.

We went to see Wolde Tsadik about a month after his surgery. We were sorry to find out that infection had set in. His leg wasn't healing as fast as the doctors thought it would. He would have to stay at Alert Hospital a while longer. We took him a tape recorder and some Bible study materials. He had already completed all seven books in our Bible correspondence series.

Since Wolde Tsadik was away from his home in Wuhay, we didn't go back to start showing filmstrips there again. We planned to do that as soon as he returned. Yet every time we visited him, we found him no nearer to being able to return home than he had been the month before. We wondered why the Lord was letting this happen.

Then we noticed something unusual. The staff kept moving him from ward to ward as bed space became available. Every time we went to see him, he had moved. We began looking for him in the room where we had last seen him, and the occupants were always able to direct us to his new quarters. Everyone knew and liked him. When we did finally find him, the room would be different, but the scene would be the same. He would be seated on a nearby bed talking to a patient with a Bible in his hand.

People come to that well-known leprosy hospital from all over Ethiopia. Many of them are Orthodox Christians. Wolde Tsadik felt a special kinship with them, and he didn't take long to introduce each one to the exciting things he had discovered in his Amharic Bible. Some of them became very interested. And so, he was moved from ward to ward, witnessing as he went. His leg didn't heal, but the Lord was using him as he was.

When we returned to Menz at the end of October, we began Bible studies again. In Kaya a group of the most faithful believers came to us with an idea. They wanted to go to Bible School—full-time. Was there any place they could go? What did we think?

Priest Girma said they wouldn't find what they were looking for at the school he attended. A lot of the teaching was devoted to church history and traditions as well as to Orthodox philosophy. They just wanted to learn the Bible. A few of them were married and had families, and everyone had land to farm and relatives to support. None of them had any savings. The solution seemed to be for them to stay in Menz. That way they could take care of their families and keep witnessing to those around them.

In addition to the Bible, they felt the need to learn a little of what the public-school students were learning, so that they wouldn't appear so ignorant in comparison. Students are frequently critical of the Orthodox Church for having an uneducated clergy, and many have used that as an excuse to stop attending.

They also wanted to learn some English—being able to speak a few words of the language shows that you've been to school. We included elementary math and some general science in the curriculum as well. We knew that simple concepts such as, "The earth is round," and "The sun stands still and the earth moves around it," would be exciting for them to hear, even if they didn't always understand or believe us.

We offered to teach them two full days a week in addition to their regular Sunday Bible studies. If we took turns teaching the entire day, they could learn quite a lot. They liked the idea, and so we began the next week. We also enlisted Priest Girma to help teach. He knew his Bible very well, and he understood the Orthodox background of all the students. He was aware of exactly what the problem areas were because he had already worked through them in his own life. We received a blessing, and our knowledge and understanding grew as we listened to him teach each day.

Tatuk was one of the first Bible students at our tent class in Kaya. It wasn't long before he began bringing his two brothers, who were also deacons. He wanted them to share what he had discovered. Abbee was Tatuk's older brother, but he was much shyer. He attended our TEE courses and did the best he could on the homework and quizzes, but it was difficult for him. He had a hard time writing answers to the questions each week, and often he didn't have time to do it at all. He was very busy as a husband and a father.

We had to choose a place to meet that would be central and convenient. We could have set up the big tent, but we didn't really need that much space. Also, the tent was cold when the wind blew, and the ground was often damp. Abbee had just built a new home in his compound that was bigger and nicer than his old one. He hadn't yet put in the door or window, but aside from that, it was finished. He offered to let us use it. It turned out to be an ideal meeting place. He continued to live in his old house for many months, and we met in his new one.

We taught on a regular basis all during the fall and early winter months. Occasionally someone new dropped in and stayed awhile, but it was the original dozen faithful deacons whom we could count on seeing every day. On Sundays the room was full. They now took charge of much of the service. Two of them preached every week, and others led the singing, passed out the songbooks and Bibles, and welcomed the visitors. Their job was to encourage each latecomer to find a seat on the grass-strewn floor once the mud benches around the wall were filled. If a priest or older adult came, someone was sure to rise and give up his seat on the bench. When it was time to look up a song number or Bible verse, there was always plenty of help for those who had trouble locating it.

All during these months, they grew skilled at using their Bibles and gained considerable knowledge. Their growth was very evident—but they didn't grow significantly in numbers. We were a little puzzled and didn't understand why. We remembered how we had prayed for one believer and the Lord had answered. Then we claimed forty believers and the Lord had again been faithful. Since that time, we had made no such specific claims.

In January our missionaries met for our annual prayer retreat. As we prayed together, the Lord convicted us that we needed to go out on a limb and pray for a multitude of new believers. This time we didn't set a limit. Excitement generated in us as we waited to see how God would answer.

Witnesses

One of those listening was a woman from the city of Thyatira named Lydia, a dealer in purple cloth. She was a worshiper of God. The Lord opened her heart to respond to Paul's message. When she and the members of her household were baptized, she invited us to her home. "If you consider me a believer in the Lord," she said, "come and stay at my house." And she persuaded us.

Acts 16:14–15

Our return from the mission prayer retreat coincided with the season for religious holidays. On Saint Mary's day in Tsahai Sina, we saw Wolde Tsadik's sister and brother. After warmly greeting us, they asked if we would please come and visit their family again, even though Wolde Tsadik wasn't there.

We realized it had been more than half a year since we had last been to their house. It was hard to believe. So much had happened during that time, and it had passed so quickly. We promised we would come, wondering what we would find when we got there. How could they possibly stay strong in their faith? With Wolde Tsadik gone, only his mother and two sisters remained who knew Jesus, and they had precious little Bible knowledge. It was almost inevitable that they would slip back into their old ways.

The whole family was standing outside their compound watching for us when we drove up. The old mother was radiant. After exchanging kisses of greeting, she began eagerly telling us what had been happening to them. She didn't even wait until we went inside and got settled. When she put her faith in Jesus and asked us to destroy all her charms, the whole neighborhood heard about it. They figured two things would happen to her.

First of all, the devil would punish her. Some catastrophe would befall the family—sickness, crop failure, an accident, a bad market for pottery, or even death. They sat back and watched to see which it would be. Secondly, they surmised that she would be sorry for her hasty behavior and would go back to the *tenkway* to get new charms. She would surely come to her senses before long.

All during the rains and the war, the family had devotions every evening. Wolde Tsadik read from the Bible and then explained what it meant. They prayed and sang together. Even the small children joined in the singing. They didn't try to hide what they were doing. All their neighbors could hear. Wolde Tsadik went away to the hospital, but that didn't put a stop to their nightly habit. Wolde Tsadik's older brother, Ayenachow, had been as far as the second grade, and he could read a little. The rest could sing and pray. And so, they kept on, and the neighbors continued to watch them.

Six months passed. It was becoming apparent that Satan wasn't going to retaliate. Not only hadn't they been bothered by him, but they were better off than they ever had been. The mother had been almost crippled by arthritis the previous year. It was no longer troubling her. Pottery prices had been at rock bottom, and now they were good. The harvest had been excellent. No one had suffered so much as a simple cold during the rains or the cold winter months. God was taking good care of them. They took advantage of every opportunity to tell their neighbors about it.

When the mother finished her story, Sinkay—her oldest son's wife—had something she wanted to ask us. She admitted having watched the three women very closely all these months. She had come to the conclusion that what they had was real. Having decided that, she wanted to know if she could pray like they had and have the same peace and joy in her life. And so, we bowed our heads together once again. Sinkay, her husband, and then Ayenachow poured out their hearts to God. An indescribably sweet sensation of joy swept over us as they became our brothers and sisters in Christ.

Before we arose to leave, Ayenachow hesitatingly asked if we thought anything could be done about a sore he had on his leg. He uncovered an oozing spot on his thigh and showed it to us. When we asked how long it had been this way, he said that it began when he was only four years old. Now he was twenty-four. He had suffered with it for twenty years! He had tried the government clinic in Mehal Meda. There he received a series of shots over a period of weeks, but they had no effect on his leg. It continued to ache and occasionally swelled. When this happened, he would be bedridden for as long as two months.

Then he went to the *tenkway*. There was at least a chance that it would do some good. The *tenkway* unhesitatingly assured him he could handle the matter. But first there was the business of payment. He asked him to bring a chicken in return for his services. When Ayenachow agreed and provided payment, he still didn't get any better. The *tenkway* said stronger medicine was needed. This time he ordered a sheep in payment. That was an expensive item, but it would be worth it to be well, so Ayenachow complied with his request. Sadly, however, there was still no change in his condition. Then the *tenkway* played his trump card. He demanded a "foreign" sheep—one of the offspring of our mission breeding program. There weren't many of them, and due to their size and scarcity, they were expensive.

But Ayenachow really wanted to be healed. It would be worth almost any price. He did everything possible to gather enough money to pay for one of these special sheep. Finally, he had enough money to buy one. He took it to the *tenkway*, eagerly anticipating his healing. How bitterly disappointed he was as the days passed and there was absolutely no improvement in his leg.

Now he asked us, "Do you think God can do anything for my leg?" As we listened to his story, we felt this was a case where healing would bring glory to God. We prayed with them that the Lord would heal Ayenachow's leg and demonstrate to all around that He is more powerful than the *tenkway*.

On Thursday, Ayenachow made the long walk to the Tsahai Sina clinic. Sam diagnosed his trouble as osteomysis of the bone. His bones were decaying inside his leg and sloughing off through the break in his skin. Such cases are rare in the United States, and they certainly aren't left untreated for twenty years. Sam and Muko prayed for him and then gave him a massive dose of penicillin, telling him to come back the following week for another shot. Within a month his leg was completely healed, and it never gave him any more trouble while we were there. Once more, those living in Wuhay saw proof that God had succeeded where the power of Satan had failed.

They asked us to start showing filmstrips at their house again. This time the sisters went from door to door, inviting their neighbors. The response was just as good as it had been before. Deacons who regularly went with us took turns preaching after the film showings.

After a few weeks the family asked when we could come to sing and pray. They wanted to learn some new songs and to have time for prayers. We had one free hour remaining in our Sunday schedule. It was when we returned from Kaya before we went to their house to show filmstrips. We volunteered to go straight to their house from Kaya, thus giving us an extra hour with them. They happily agreed.

We arrived at their home just at dusk each week, and the light of a single kerosene wick lantern scarcely punctuated the gloom. In that semi-darkness, it was impossible to tell who anyone was as people came in with white robes tightly wrapped around them against the chilly night air. For a long time, I had prided myself on being able to tell who was praying, just by the sound of their voice. But now as we prayed, we often heard unfamiliar voices. People came in while our heads were bowed and joined in prayer when they felt led by God. We heard many come to know Jesus personally through prayer, but we won't know who they are until our spirits recognize each other in heaven. We are thankful there will be no darkness there.

Sundays were filled with singing. They loved it! Every place we met, they sang. The church at Sar Midir invited us to begin teaching the Bible there. Ray preached and I taught, and the response was excellent. Then we went to Kaya to spend the afternoon. Since everyone walked to get there, they were ready to stay awhile. A typical service lasted three hours and included two or three sermons. After finishing there we went to Wuhay. As we traveled from place to place, a lot of our friends accompanied us. Our Land Rover was always packed to the limit the springs would bear. We made sure that all had equal chances to go.

We kept a box of Bibles and a box of songbooks in the car. We were usually scarcely on our way before someone would pass out the song books and announce a number. Then they would start singing. They sang at the top of their lungs in spite of the fact that there were often fifteen of us crowded in the car. They wanted to be heard over the racket of the engine. Most of all, they enjoyed making a joyful noise to the Lord.

When there were no books on hand, or when we were traveling in the dark, they sang the songs they knew by heart. Some were simple tunes with numerous verses. When these ran out, they used their imaginations and made up more. All told, we spent four hours on the road every Sunday—if we didn't get stuck in the mud or have car trouble. But the time passed quickly as we fellowshipped and sang together.

Sometimes the road got too rough or steep. Then we all climbed out and ran alongside the Land Rover until it got better again. When we got stuck in the mud, everyone helped carry rocks to pile in the hole left by the tire when the car was jacked up. When we got enough rocks, we all helped push. We even had fun getting muddy together. They discovered there is a special joy in just being with Christian brothers. It didn't matter what they were doing.

The Fire Spreads

Paul entered the synagogue and spoke boldly there for three months, arguing persuasively about the kingdom of God. But some of them became obstinate; they refused to believe and publicly maligned the Way. So Paul left them. He took the disciples with him and had discussions daily in the lecture hall of Tyrannus. This went on for two years, so that all the Jews and Greeks who lived in the province of Asia heard the word of the Lord.

Acts 19:8–10

After the prayer retreat, we not only returned to our friends' house in Wuhay, but we also went to Abbee's house in Kaya. It felt wonderful to be back with our friends again. They had planned to meet every Sunday of our three-week absence, but the last Sunday no one had shown up. We had been concerned for several months that the group seemed to have stopped growing. We asked them what they thought the problem was.

As was often the case, Girma spoke for all of them. On the second Sunday we were gone, they carefully looked over those in attendance. A head count showed that almost everyone attending was from Akafee—over an hour's walk away from Abbee's house. It would obviously be easier for them to meet closer to home. In addition, they had some friends who had expressed an interest, but they were unwilling to walk that far just to see. They might come if there were a more central location.

Girma tentatively suggested using the tent again. Then we could meet in Akafee. His house was right at the edge of the *amudgway*, the big grazing area, and he thought we could get there in our Land Rover. He offered to let us set up camp in his yard if we wanted to give it a try.

The other students immediately seconded his idea, so we moved. On our very first day there, nearly a hundred people came for classes. Some of them were from Digimsha, an area on past Akafee. We were amazed at the response, but we figured the novelty would soon wear off. We were wrong. As the weeks passed, they continued to come.

After our tent became rotted and ripped, we got a new one. We set it up in Girma's compound. It was big enough as a central meeting room, but we didn't have enough classrooms for so many students, so we set up the old one too. Since it was the dry season, the holes didn't matter. All that was needed was a little shade and a windbreak. It was fine for that purpose.

Girma gladly let one group meet inside his home. In addition, there were remains of a house on the lower half of his compound. The walls were still partially standing, and it was possible to drape a tarp over it to serve as a roof. That gave us four classrooms. We divided the people into the same number of groups: women, shepherd children, beginning Bible students, and advanced Bible learners.

The next problem was teachers. Priest Girma still came every morning, even though he had to walk a considerable distance now that we had moved. He taught each of the groups in turn. But Ray and I couldn't do everything else. It was just more than we could handle. The Lord knew our needs and supplied the logical solution. We graduated the young men whom we had been training so intensively for the past year and a half, and they became the teachers.

As we observed them, we saw that they succeeded in situations that were difficult for us. The women who had started coming were so bound by tradition that they found it hard to learn from a foreigner. They were so distracted by how I looked that they couldn't pay attention to what I was saying. Sometimes I covered my face with my *gabi* so that they couldn't see me when I talked. That helped, but communication was still difficult.

Mispronouncing just one syllable in a word sometimes caused them to lose the meaning of an entire sentence. Then too, their lives as peasant women were so different from mine. It was hard for me to find examples in teaching that they could relate to. The young shepherd children were little better. We found that it took endless repetition before they began to retain anything.

We had been spoiled. We had grown accustomed to teaching quick learners who grasped our ideas even when we couldn't find the right words to express them. Our new teachers didn't share any of our problems. Their accents and word usage were perfect. They had just the right Menz voice. They were Menzies and they knew what illustrations in teaching had hit home when they were first learning. In short, they were the ideal teachers.

For over a year, it had become very awkward for us to attend any of the Kaya churches. There were still some people in the area who were suspicious of us. So, we camped and stayed close to the tent for our teaching. But that didn't stop the Word from spreading. Students regularly came to the tent from seven different church areas. They went home every week and faithfully shared what they had learned with their families and friends. Many even had chances to witness in their own churches.

Tests on books of the Bible and memory work began taking more and more of our time. People were coming from everywhere to take the tests. Nearly all were Orthodox priests and deacons. A big group began coming from Hanna, an area about ten miles north, where fighting had been the heaviest. They begged us to come and teach them. How we would have liked to, but we couldn't begin anything new. It was almost time for our furlough. Someone else would have to teach them.

We began to see our Bible students in a new light as they became the natural leaders of their people. They were no longer the shy self-conscious students they used to be. They had become confident young men, and they could go places that we would never be able to reach.

Girma fell naturally into the role of host at all our meetings after we set up camp in his yard. People began to look to him for help and advice.

Although he was only twenty-five and was unmarried, he had an air of maturity. He was quick to grasp spiritual truths, and he had a way of making them plain to others in his sermons.

His house was adjacent to the community *adbar* tree. Late each afternoon, the shadow of it fell on his house. One day he told the group what an influence it had been on his life. When he was still a boy, he had gotten his first sheep. After about a month it became sick. In spite of all that he did, it got worse and worse. He was afraid it was about to die. In desperation he took it to the *adbar* tree and made a vow. If his lamb survived, he would sacrifice one of its offspring to the *adbar*.

The lamb did recover and soon grew up and had a lamb of its own. It was about time for Girma to keep his promise. He feared the consequences if he didn't. But as he was preparing to fulfill his half of the bargain, we began our Bible studies for priests and deacons in Kaya. He quickly grasped the truth of what we taught and committed his life to Christ at the Mehal Meda meeting. Having made that decision, he gave up his vow to sacrifice a lamb. It wasn't necessary. He no longer had to fear the power of the *adbar*.

Tatuk was another frequent Sunday preacher. By nature, he was a quiet person of few words. But when he stood before a group with a Bible in his hand, all that changed. His messages were plain and simple and rang with a note of authority that clearly came from the Lord. People paid close attention whenever he spoke.

Priest Girma and Tatuk

Abba Asefa came to our Bible studies in Kaya right from the start. He had become a monk when his wife died six years earlier. One of his primary duties was that of reconciling people and families who had quarreled. He also had a big responsibility as a father confessor. When he came to know Jesus, he didn't give up these jobs—instead they began to acquire real meaning. He began to tell people that forgiveness is a gift of God, coming only after true repentance. It can't be bought with goods or services. As God has forgiven us, so should we forgive each other. He was in the right position to put his faith into practice.

Abba Asefa

The person who amazed us the most, though, was Aschallew. He had changed from being an impetuous hothead to being the most patient and faithful teacher of the whole group. No matter what time we arrived, we were sure to find him teaching anyone who happened to be around. He taught them songs and helped them practice Bible drills. He shared the little arithmetic he knew and drilled them on the 260-letter Amharic alphabet. He was still bold and outspoken. But now God was using those traits in making him a powerful preacher and teacher.

The most thrilling thing about Aschallew was that he had changed from being the type of person who would beat up his weaving partner, into one who was loving and self-sacrificing. It was a total transformation, and no one but God could have done it. He always kept his New Testament in his shirt pocket. Because there were no children in his family to shepherd the animals, he had to spend long hours out in the fields. While the animals grazed, he read his Bible—again and again. God inscribed the words indelibly on his mind. Before long he was almost a living concordance. Given just a few words as a clue, he could locate a verse within a minute or two—any verse. We had never seen anything like it.

In all the time we spent with them, there was only one thing we felt was lacking. Our busy Sunday schedule took us from Bible study to Bible study. They began each one the minute we arrived and continued until we had to leave. There was no time to pray together. We realized a lengthy time of prayer with the whole group in the tent wasn't the answer. Many didn't yet know Christ as savior, and besides there were far too many people. But sometime, somewhere, we needed to take enough time to really talk to God.

We had a chance one night when a large group met at the Groce's house. We studied the Bible first and then prayed and talked long into the night. It was wonderful, but we knew that was a somewhat artificial situation.

One Sunday we arrived at the tent in Kaya to find only a small group of women and children inside being taught by Aschallew. Usually there was a crowd waiting when we drove up. We wondered where everybody was. Then we walked on through the tent to greet Girma. As we stepped out into his yard, we heard voices coming from the tarp-covered enclosure. Taking a closer look, we saw a room full of bowed heads. One person was praying. When they finished, they told us that they had been meeting there for several weeks to pray together prior to our coming. They had felt the same need as we had, and they had done something about it.

Before they returned to the main tent, Wolde Aragay said he had something he wanted to share with them. As many of them already knew, in December he had gotten very sick. Since Muko had gone home to Wollamo for Christmas, he had to go to Mehal Meda to the clinic. His father lived there, and Wolde Aragay was able to stay with him. He got a lot of shots from the clinic, but he continued to get worse.

It wasn't many days before the *tenkway* came to call. In years past the *tenkway* never had to drum up business, but times were getting tougher. He didn't have as many customers as he used to. He told Wolde Aragay that he needed to have his fortune written on a piece of parchment equal to his height rolled up as a scroll and put in a leather pouch to be worn on a string around his neck. When Wolde Aragay hesitated, he became more forceful. "If you don't come to me for help now, you will die on January 16." Summoning all his courage, Wolde Aragay stood up to him and said that he didn't need any of his medicine. Jesus would take care of him. With a withering glance, the *tenkway* turned on his heels and left.

The effect on the household members was instantaneous. They began mourning as if Wolde Aragay's death was already an accomplished fact. Wails of despair filled the house as the women beat their breasts and tore their hair. How could he be so foolish! The *tenkway* was always right. Wolde Aragay was practically signing his own death warrant by refusing to cooperate.

The ten days before January 16 passed incredibly slowly, with no perceptible improvement in Wolde Aragay's condition. But neither did he get worse, and he repeatedly claimed the promise of the Bible that no one could snatch him from the Lord's hand—not even the *tenkway*. He told his relatives that Jesus was more powerful than the *tenkway* and Jesus would protect him.

Wolde Aragay had known of people who died for challenging the *tenkway*. It was not unusual for a *tenkway* to pronounce a curse, only to have the person die a short time later. He didn't underestimate the power of the man he dared to oppose, but he knew the power of Jesus. He was sure it was greater, and he was willing to stake his life on it.

January 16 finally arrived. Wolde Aragay was still sick, but he wasn't dead. People watched him anxiously all day, trying to detect any sign of impending disaster. Their worst fears were never realized. The day passed uneventfully.

The next morning Wolde Aragay woke up feeling a little better, and before long he was able to go back home to Kaya. But he still wasn't completely well. As his sickness continued, he took another good look at his life. The Lord convicted him of sin in some neglected areas. He prayed for forgiveness and cleansing. The next day he came to Bible study and asked the group to pray for him. When he woke up the following morning, he felt better than he had in six weeks. By the end of the week, he was completely well.

As Wolde Aragay told his story, he praised the Lord for both his discipline and his protection. The Lord had not only strengthened his faith, but He had caused him to be a testimony to his relatives. They had never seen anyone successfully challenge the *tenkway* before. It gave them a lot to think about.

While the prayer meetings before services in Kaya had really met a general need, the leaders there still felt the need of an occasional special prayer meeting. They had so many responsibilities and opportunities these days. When they met in April they didn't come to our house, but they had gathered in Kaya in the home of Deacon Irgutay. To make it as simple as possible, they agreed that his wife shouldn't prepare any food. Everyone could eat before they came. They planned to gather just at dusk when their day's work was done.

On the chosen evening, we hurried along the narrow, winding path carved into the steep hillside. The sun had set, and it was beginning to get dark and cold. Dogs rushed out to bark their fury at us as we passed, but they didn't bother us as long as we stayed out of their territory. We greeted many tired farmers on their way home after a long day in the fields. With so much activity around us, our mile-long walk was over before we knew it.

When we arrived at Irgutay's home, a number of our friends were already there. In honor of the occasion, they had spread new *gooz gwaz* (tall green grass) all over the floor. It gave a sweet fresh smell to everything. Two small kerosene lamps lent a mellow glow to the shadowy atmosphere. Soon everyone was there, and the large round room was full.

An hour or two was spent in Bible study and singing, but most of the time was reserved for testimonies of the Lord's working in their lives and for prayer. They wanted to be sure of the Lord's leading in the days ahead, and they were also very burdened for their fellow Orthodox who didn't know a living God. It was midnight before they were ready to stop.

We were expecting to leave when we finished praying, but before we could get up, they brought out some food. On their own they had gotten together and decided they wanted to share a meal. They had divided up the responsibility and each had brought a little. They set out several large baskets of *injera* and *wat* and we clustered around them. As we each tore off a piece of the *injera* with our right hand and dipped it in the *wat* in the middle, we felt a precious bond of kinship. Eating together was such a natural thing to do. We were truly a family.

Most of them stayed there and slept on the floor for the night. We chose to return to our own beds in the tent. We took our flashlight, and with Girma, Aschallew, and Seedelel as escorts, we made our way back along the rock path to our campsite by Girma's house. We were lighthearted as we talked together on the way. God had filled all of us to overflowing with His goodness. We didn't even notice the cold.

To the Ends of the Earth

"But you will receive power when the Holy Spirit comes on you; and you will be my witnesses in Jerusalem, and in all Judea and Samaria, and to the ends of the earth."

Acts 1:8

Although we spent a lot of time teaching the Bible, community development wasn't forgotten. It was an integral part of everything we did. We always carried simple medicines to help people out between clinics. Women in a number of places were practicing using carding combs. One young woman in Tsahai Sina was getting pretty good at using the spinning wheel. We frequently hauled sheep or chickens to be sold for breeding. And we still had rug markets every month.

Lynn and Ray helped clean up several springs—separating the areas where the animals came to drink from those where the women drew their water. Akafee Church even asked Ray to design a cement wall around their holy spring so that the water wouldn't be contaminated. The men of the church worked together with him all one day on its construction.

But the most exciting project was the development of the flax industry. Most Menz farmers already grow flax. Their wives like to use the seeds in *wat*. They even make an unusual drink of the mashed seeds.

But they don't know that linseed oil can be extracted from the seeds, or that there is a tough fiber hidden inside the stems.

This fiber has been used for centuries in other parts of the world to make linen—a very durable cloth. Those living in Menz only know that the stems are not good as hay, and they can't be fed to animals. They are too stiff to be used to hold plaster together and they prick your feet if you try to work them into the mud. They don't even burn good.

Lynn began experimenting with better varieties of flax. The flax grown in Menz is stunted and grow only to about a foot in height. In his sample plot he grew some varieties that were over three feet tall. Also, the average Menz yield is about four to one—giving them four times as much seed back as they plant. Some of the new varieties of seed yielded twenty to one.

The experiments were conducted under the exact same conditions that Menz farmers face at ten thousand feet: frigid nights, constant wind, not enough rain, depleted soil, and no fertilizer. If the plants didn't survive all of this, they would be of no use in Menz. Lynn used wheat, barley, and flax seeds that had already been tested at high altitudes. When the crops were ready, we held a farm demonstration day. Everyone was invited to come and see for themselves. They were very impressed as they walked around the sample plots. Never had they seen such plants before.

Then Ray showed them how to remove the flax seeds without destroying the stems. A box with nails driven in it that tapered to a spout at one end made quick work of it. After that he brought out some flax fiber and spun it into a rope. He challenged them to break it. Even with several people pulling at each end, it held firm. They were anxious to find out the secret. Where had the mysterious fiber come from?

Ray carefully described the age-old process. First the stems have to be soaked. It takes over a month in the cold climate of Menz. When the stems begin to rot, they are laid out to dry. Finally, in true Menz fashion, they are placed in a heap and beaten with *doolas*. As the chaff breaks off the outside of the stem, the thin tough fiber emerges. That was as far as he had to go. They knew what to do with fibers. Every boy learns at an early age how to make string and rope, and every girl acquires the art of spinning cotton or wool. The flax thread can be woven into cloth or sacking in the same way as they already weave cotton.

Another thing that we were really anxious to teach them to do was to irrigate. Their farming is solely dependent on rainfall. Much of the year they can't farm at all. There is more than enough water in the rainy season, but it always floods uncontrolled down the hillsides, eroding the land. None of the water is ever dammed or saved.

Every time we drove to Addis, we passed two lush valleys that were irrigated simply by means of gravity flow irrigation canals leading from small streams. A tiny creek keeps a whole valley green all year around. But Menzies are by nature suspicious of their neighbors. An irrigation canal would have to cross many people's lands. It would mean cooperation. They feared that one man might get more than his share of the water. We tried to get people to agree upon one of the several choice spots, but we had no luck. They just weren't ready for it yet.

As time passed in Menz, we discovered something interesting. We had known from the beginning that our community development program gave us access to new areas. Wherever we went we always found a few who took an interest in anything we had to teach. But largely it was an uphill battle—getting them to see the advantages of switching to better ways of doing things.

Now that was all changing. Those who had accepted Christ into their lives began wanting to improve their living conditions. They were trying to take better care of their families. They were interested in progress and were willing to try new things. If we said something would help them, they took us at our word. We had never deceived them yet. So, they were the ones to try out our seeds and buy our breeding animals. After watching them, their neighbors dared to follow along.

Kaya wasn't the only area where young men were maturing as leaders. There was also a good group of students in Tsahai Sina. Most of them, however, were either older with heavy responsibilities at home and church, or younger and not really mature enough for leadership yet.

Haile Giorgis was a notable exception. When he first started coming to Bible studies, he came only as a cautious observer. He was very traditional and was extremely loyal to his church. As he listened, he turned over every new idea in his mind, carefully examining it from all sides.

Haile Giorgis was an excellent Bible student and came in time to know our living Lord. Because he was the best preacher in the Tsahai Sina group, he often got the chance to preach at church and at Thursday clinics. When he spoke, he always wore a white cloth wrapped around his head, identifying himself as an Orthodox Church leader. We knew him for over a year before we discovered that he was not from Menz. His home was in Boruna, four days walk away. He had come to Tsahai Sina five years earlier to its well-known school for training priests, and he had stayed on as a rug weaver.

Living in Tsahai Sina was not our own choice when we began mission work in Menz, but it soon became obvious that the Lord had a hand in it. One of the best priest training schools in all of Menz was practically on our doorstep. Many of the deacons in training came to our Bible studies and we began to discover that they came from all over—even from areas outside Menz. We couldn't have been more strategically located.

Haile Giorgis shared a dream with us one day. He wanted us to go to Boruna with him and teach the Bible there. He would like it best if we would come and live there, but if we couldn't do that, he would like us to at least make a visit. He told us that there was already an airstrip there and that a passenger plane came once a week from Addis. He wondered if our mission plane could take us there from Menz.

The only problem he could see in relation to our going would be that no one would be expecting us. The airstrip was three hours walk from his house and we would have to carry everything without any help. Also, we wanted to go during the week so that we wouldn't have to cancel our Sunday classes. He thought it would be more difficult to gather people together on a weekday. But a midweek visit was better than none, so we made tentative arrangements.

At our next mission Executive Committee meeting, it was agreed that Ray and I should go to Boruna on a survey trip. We checked with MAF to see if and when they could fly us. They said they were familiar with the strip and would be willing to go there. The first available date was on a Monday, four weeks away. They could come back and get us on the following Friday in connection with a clinic trip.

We were eager to get back to Menz to tell Haile Giorgis the news. We knew how excited he would be. Our mission had given their approval on Thursday, and we arranged the flights on the next day. We drove back to Menz on Saturday, knowing we would see Haile Giorgis at Bible study on Sunday. We were anxious to give him the good word, but he didn't come. We knew he must have a good reason as he rarely missed class.

Early the next morning he came knocking at our door. With him was an old man we didn't know. Beaming, Haile Giorgis introduced his father. He had just arrived the day before from Boruna. Haile Giorgis had been living in Tsahai Sina for five years, and this was the very first time anyone from Boruna had ever come to visit him. It was not only an extremely difficult and tiring trip, but it was actually dangerous in some places.

We asked his father what had prompted him to come at this particular time. He told us that he had no special reason. On Thursday he just got an unexplainable urge to go and visit his son. So, he set out, not even knowing the route—only the general direction. He asked for help along the way and arrived on Sunday afternoon. Again, for some unknown reason, Haile Giorgis hadn't accompanied us to Kaya that day, so he was at home when his dad arrived. God's hand was very evident to us.

We told both of them our plans to visit Boruna in exactly four weeks. Haile Giorgis was ecstatic. He could hardly wait. He and his father eagerly made plans and then Haile Giorgis wrote notes to the priests and community leaders telling them that we would be coming. We would also be bringing films to show if they wanted to schedule any meetings. Then, with the arrangements complete, less than twenty-four hours after his arrival, his father turned around and headed back home. Inside his shirt he had our special delivery letters. The details of our trip could not have been taken care of in a better way.

The day of the journey soon arrived, and we drove to Mehal Meda to meet the plane. We were happy to see it when it landed as we were eagerly anticipating the trip. The pilot told us he had received an emergency call after he was in the air, but because he was already on his way to get us, he didn't turn back.

Haile Giorgis's eyes grew wide as he got in the small plane and it raced down the strip, churning up clouds of dust behind it. Suddenly it rose in the air. Everything below got smaller and smaller, but the details were still quite distinct. The pilot had never been to Boruna before, so he took a compass reading from his map and set his direction. He would fly on that course for twenty-eight minutes, and that should put us there.

Haile Giorgis kept his eyes focused on the ground. He kept pointing out landmarks along the path he had traveled when he first came to Menz, and again on his two trips home to visit. But then the path turned. It made a big detour, and the plane continued straight. From that point on, everything looked strange to Haile Giorgis. After twenty-five minutes, the pilot asked him if he recognized anything. Try as he might, he couldn't find a single familiar landmark. Two more minutes ticked past. Finally, after thirty minutes of flying, Haile Giorgis spotted the capital of Boruna up the hill from the strip. It was dead ahead, and we were right on course.

When we landed, his father and brothers ran to meet us. In their eagerness not to miss us, they had been out waiting since dawn. Unloading our things, the pilot promised to return in four days—providing that it didn't rain too much, and the strip was dry. Then he taxied off.

We traveled light, taking only one change of clothes apiece and lightweight sleeping bags. But they insisted we bring Bibles to give out and the projector plus a car battery. Before we agreed, we had made them practice carrying the fifty-pound battery at our house. They assured us that two men could carry it without difficulty by putting their *doolas* through the handles of its wooden case and shouldering them.

Now they insisted on carrying the rest of our things as well, and we set off. By this time, it was late morning, and the sun was beaming down full force. There wasn't a cloud in the sky. Boruna is only at seven thousand feet and is consequently much warmer than Menz. The path would endlessly uphill. When we finally got to the top of the ridge, we immediately started down the other side. Then came another mountain. We wondered if we would ever get there.

Many of the people in Boruna are Orthodox Christians, the same as in Menz. But there are also a lot of Moslems and when we passed the areas where they lived, our friends pointed them out. As we walked along, we kept an eye out for a possible site for a future landing strip, but we didn't have any luck. There was no place big enough or flat enough.

Even though they were carrying everything, Haile Giorgis and his relatives had to wait for us to catch up several times. When we finally arrived at their house, we figured we had walked seven miles. In that distance we had climbed 1,000 feet, gone back down 1,500 feet, and then climbed 500 feet again.

The houses in Boruna are large and rectangular and are very different from the small round houses of Menz. The roof has a peak and is open on one end since there is no problem with cold. All the animals are stabled in the entry area of the house at night. When it came time to go to bed, they invited us to lie down alongside everyone else in the central area near the fire. Just beyond the chest-high partition in the room were two oxen, a horse, a cow, two goats, eight sheep, and some chickens. To go outside after dark or before dawn, you must work your way through the animals, being careful to watch where you step. We experienced culture shock as we were forced to elbow our way between the rump of a horse and the horns of a bull.

We expressed our wish to sleep by ourselves in the back end of the house, where they prepared and stored their food. After a few protests, they finally agreed, and we settled down for the night. It was raining, and we could see the sky through a hole in the thatch directly overhead. We soon discovered that the roof leaked all over in this little room. As we squirmed to avoid the largest drips, we were continually conscious of the animals and people sleeping nearby. We spent a fitful night that seemed as if it would never end. Mercifully, morning finally came. The next night they spread straw on the dirt floor for us to sleep on, and it stopped raining before we went to bed. We settled down and never heard another thing all night.

Haile Giorgis's parents were gracious hosts and tried to anticipate our every need. In addition to all they fed us, we ate in every house we visited. Haile Giorgis was much loved, and he was welcomed with open arms by everyone he met. They were glad he was back from his long years of deacon training. He introduced us to everyone and told his friends that they could trust us. We had come to help them and to teach them about Jesus. As a result, wherever we went, we had a chance to witness. We showed Bible filmstrips every evening in different homes and each time their houses were packed.

Wednesday turned out to be a religious holiday, so everyone went to church. Because Haile Giorgis vouched for us, they included us without question. In one day, we felt the same degree of acceptance as we had achieved in Menz after living there for seven years. It was amazing. After the service they asked Ray to preach and then Haile Giorgis was given a turn.

We assured them that Haile Giorgis knew his Bible well and was a good preacher. Because we were foreigners, they respected us. With our endorsement, they were willing to listen to him, even though he was still a young man. He preached after each filmstrip as well as at church that day, and he witnessed every time he got a chance. He gained authority by being there with us that would have taken him years to acquire if he had simply returned on his own after deacon training.

After the service, we gave Bibles to the church leaders and tracts to everyone else. Then the priests invited us to sit with them and share some bread. All during the four days that we were in Boruna, many left their work and took time to visit and study with us.

Although the people in Boruna were somewhat more advanced than those in Menz, we still saw a lot of ways that we could help. They badly needed medical care. Although their climate is not as hostile as Menz, they could use some help in farming. The area would be ideal for irrigation, and several were anxious to try. They were having some problems with sickness in their animals. A veterinarian would be a big help.

We soon discovered that their Christianity was just as intertwined with devil worship as that in Menz. The *adbar* tree cast a shadow over everything they did and the *tenkways* were powerful and influential. There was so much that we could do. We began to wonder if we might be able to work in this area too. They eagerly offered us all kinds of cooperation and help, as well as a place to live, if we would consider it.

All too soon, it was time to leave. Late Thursday afternoon we made the long hike back to town. Because the plane was coming early in the morning, we needed to spend the night near the strip. We stayed in the house of an old family friend. He used to teach Haile Giorgis and the other deacons in the priest school in Tsahai Sina. After he learned rug weaving from us, he moved back to Boruna to teach. His wife was one of my favorite students in the ladies' class. She fixed a delicious meal, and we spent a pleasant evening reminiscing about old times and mutual friends.

That afternoon we had walked around the town and had been introduced to several church leaders. We had a brief opportunity to get acquainted with them, and they, too, expressed a desire for us to come and teach there.

In the morning we hiked back to the strip and finished clearing off some rocks as the pilot had requested. Then we sat down to wait. It had rained a little each day, except for the last night. Right now, the strip was dry and he should have no trouble landing. We felt like we had just made a journey into another world. The arrival of the plane and a chance to talk to the pilot brought us back down to earth. We were glad he had come to get us, but we hoped that we would get a chance to return someday.

Arrest

When the seven days were nearly over, some Jews from the province of Asia saw Paul at the temple. They stirred up the whole crowd and seized him, shouting, "Fellow Israelites, help us! This is the man who teaches everyone everywhere against our people and our law and this place. And besides, he has brought Greeks into the temple and defiled this holy place." (They had previously seen Trophimus the Ephesian in the city with Paul and assumed that Paul had brought him into the temple.)

Acts 21:27–29

When we began our extension seminary program in the fall, we promised the most faithful students a trip to Addis at the end of the year. Many of them had never been out of Menz. They wanted to see the wonders of the big city as well as the best of the Orthodox Church. More importantly, they would be able to make the acquaintance of some Christian brothers. We missionaries, and the few evangelists who had come to Menz, were the only born-again believers they knew, outside of their own group. It was time to expand their vision.

The first weekend in May was set aside for the big trip. Eleven deacons came with Priest Girma on Thursday evening to spend the night at our house so that we could get an early start the next morning. Wolde Tsadik would join us in Addis. He was still at the leprosy hospital and was at last being fitted with an artificial leg.

We drove two Land Rovers, stopping to visit spots of interest enroute. They saw a cave full of mummies, with their teeth and hair still intact. We traveled along the continental divide at twelve thousand feet, where water on one side of the road flows to the Red Sea and on the other side to the Mediterranean. They caught a glimpse of the Danakil Desert—much of it below sea level. And of course, we showed them the two lush, irrigated valleys fed only by small streams.

Finally, we arrived in the capitol city of Addis Ababa. Their eyes were bright as they tried to take in a multitude of sights. There were cars going in every direction and lights shining all day. Blinking neon signs and television vied for their attention. Tall buildings were on every corner. They walked through a supermarket filled with everything imaginable and rode in a twelve-story glass elevator. When they visited the lion cages, they were rewarded with a royal roar. They even took turns talking to each other on the mission telephone. There was no end to the wonders of the city.

Ray and I had some new experiences as well. We found a restaurant that served hot meals for only 25 cents per person. Unfortunately, it was necessary to walk through a bar to get to the dining room. We overheard some pretty choice comments when the patrons noticed that the group included a woman, and a foreigner at that. But the food was good, and the price was right, so we went back. One day we were across town in the market area at mealtime. We all ate in a restaurant where the going rate for all you could eat was only 12½ cents! It was hard to believe, considering how high food prices were in grocery stores. What's more, it tasted good.

But all these diversions didn't cause us to forget our primary purpose in visiting Addis. On Saturday morning we visited Holy Trinity Cathedral. Isaias, their teacher from the Rainy Season Bible School, worked in an office nearby. Seeing him again was almost like a family reunion. He escorted us to the cathedral and accompanied us as a priest gave us a grand tour.

Holy Trinity is a priceless treasury of Ethiopian art. There are intricate stained-glass windows and giant paintings on the walls and ceilings. Ornate tombs of past emperors and empresses hold a special place of honor. We were even admitted to the room where all the crowns and coronation robes of previous royalty are stored and displayed. Their beauty is breathtaking. We visited several other Orthodox churches that morning. Each was unique and had its own special points of interest. An old monk in long robes unlocked one historic church for us. After we all stepped inside, he bolted the door behind him. There was no question as to the beauty of the churches we visited, but signs of life were scarce.

Before we ever left Menz, we prayed with our fellow missionaries and our countryside friends about the wisdom of taking them to Addis while there was still political unrest. Arrest of dissidents was by now a fairly common occurrence. Off and on in recent months, there had been trouble in Addis. We didn't want to take them to the city and expose them to danger. But we had promised them the trip, and we knew they would enjoy it. We finally decided it was worth the risk.

As we planned our weekend activities, we were told there was a good evangelical prayer meeting on Saturday afternoon that we could attend. We had heard about the group before, but we had never been to one of their services. They had been the target of persecution for a number of years. Many of their members had spent some time in jail.

Since the change in government, they had encountered fewer problems. The powerful Orthodox Church was no longer opposing them as a rival group. It was too busy fighting for its own existence. The *Abuna* had recently been deposed and placed under arrest and a new one had been appointed by the government in his place.

A friend gave us directions as to the time and place of the meeting. When we got there, I jumped out of the car I was driving. Ray suggested I go on in and check to be sure we were in the right place before everyone else got out. I threaded my way through the crowd outside and entered the compound. Sure enough, there was the large tent we had been told to look for. As I approached it, a young man came up and grabbed my arms.

"You're under arrest!" he announced defiantly. Sensing my confusion, he went on. "Didn't you see the sign outside declaring that this church is illegal? You're one of the people who comes here all the time. I know you're trying to undermine Ethiopia. This church is bad for the country. Politics and religion just don't mix. You can't love God and love Ethiopia too." Since he spoke to me in English, I answered him in the same language. I assured him that we had never been to that church before and that this was our first visit.

At that point Ray decided to find out why I hadn't returned. As he approached the gate, they warned him that if he entered, he would be placed under arrest too. Concerned for the two cars full of young men in our care, I urged him to go back. As he went, part of the angry mob followed him. Belligerently, they insinuated we were CIA agents and illegal entries. They threatened to hang us. All the while, they talked against God and the church. They wanted all the Bibles of the young men in our cars. They said they were going to destroy them.

Meanwhile, a crowd gathered around me. They accused us of taking advantage of the Ethiopian people, especially those poor country peasants they could see in our cars. They blamed Ethiopia's present troubles on the influence of foreigners like us. As they were railing at me, I heard one young man tell another in Amharic, "If she says she hasn't been here before, it's true. Those kinds of Christians never lie." I marveled at his inadvertent testimony.

I stood there with my head bowed, asking God to take control of the situation. One of my captors asked me what I was doing. "Are you praying?" he queried. "It won't do a bit of good. There is no God." For thirty minutes they held on to my arms and kept me there, the object of insults and abuse. And then, inexplicably, they ordered me to leave. I didn't wait to be told twice. As I hurried to the car, I was tempted to point out that prayer did work after all, but I felt it was time for a little discretion. I was anxious to escape before they changed their minds. As we pulled away from the angry mob, they tugged at the door handles and banged on the car frames, all the while hurling insults until we were out of sight.

The young men with us had seen and heard it all. They knew the accusations were false. A year earlier we had distributed copies of *Tortured for Christ* by Richard Wurmbrand in Amharic. They read it but said that it didn't really make sense to them. In particular, they didn't understand the meaning of "communism." They had asked us to explain, and we did our best. But they still couldn't grasp the idea. It was just too alien a concept.

Now God had accomplished in half an hour what we hadn't been able to do in months of teaching. There was no doubt in their minds about what they had just witnessed. We learned later that the local people's association had met and arbitrarily decided to take over the church that met in the tent and its buildings. They didn't pay anything for it; they just took possession. There was no court of appeals where anyone could protest such action. Under the new political setup, the local association had become a law in itself, and there was no recourse against its decisions. The members were no longer allowed to gather in their church. Freedom of religion was beginning to disappear.

On Sunday morning, we rose early and made our way to a big holiday celebration at one of the well-known Orthodox churches in Addis. Thousands milled in the courtyard while mass was in progress inside. The pathway was cluttered with beggars exposing their diseases and infirmities, begging for alms in the name of the patron saint of the day. As we drew closer to the church building, we saw dozens of ornate umbrellas, one after the other, being passed forward through the crowd as offerings to the church. After being displayed, they were taken inside. It was an impressive sight. In the press of the crowd, it was impossible to get close enough to either see or hear any of the service, so we decided to leave.

We went from there to a Baptist mission chapel. Its members were just gathering when we arrived. They had heard of God's work among our Orthodox friends, and they welcomed them warmly as brothers in Christ. They were introduced as special guests in the service, and when some familiar songs were sung, they felt right at home.

As soon as that service was finished, we went to another church that had originally begun with the help of missionaries but was now indigenous. The preacher was well into his message when we arrived, but we squeezed in and settled down to listen anyway. I don't know how much we missed, but we got there for over an hour of his sermon!

He recounted the story of how thirty Christian brothers had been arrested Friday night and had been thrown in jail. They had been attending the church in the tent when it was declared illegal. Our friends were electrified. They knew exactly what he was talking about. They had been there and they had seen it with their own eyes. As he told of the persecution, he predicted that many of those listening would soon be forced to stand up for their faith in a similar way and he challenged them to be spiritually prepared.

After the benediction, they announced that it was a special day of fasting and prayer. They invited any who wanted, to stay for an afternoon meeting. Our friends were eager to accept the invitation. This is what they had come to Addis for—to be with other Christians. They asked us if they could remain. We were as glad for the chance as they were.

After more Bible study and a season of prayer, the church leaders announced that they were going to observe the Lord's Supper. First, they came over and spoke to our Orthodox friends. They assured them that they accepted them as brothers in Christ and that they were welcome to partake of the Lord's Supper if they wanted. It was entirely up to them. Our friends were touched by the spirit of fellowship and acceptance they felt, but they were still members of the Orthodox Church and they wanted to continue to be. They felt like they had a mission to their fellow church members. They knew that a single false step could ruin everything. The case of the donkey meat accusation was still fresh in their minds. After talking it over, they agreed that as long as they belonged to the Orthodox Church, they would abide by its rules.

It wasn't the first time such a discussion had come up. Twice before we had seriously talked about baptism: once when Priest Girma went with us to see the baptism of some of our own children, and again when a group of deacons from Kaya came inquiring about secret baptism in our bathtub. We discussed it for a long time. Doing anything in secret meant taking the responsibility of deciding who could be trusted to be let in on the secret. One weak person or a spy could ruin everything. That is what had happened to the evangelical group in Addis. They had been betrayed several times by members in their midst.

We were convinced that baptism was an important element in Christian obedience. They had all been baptized in the Orthodox Church as babies, but they had not been baptized again after the change that occurred in their lives when they placed their faith in Jesus Christ.

The real issue at stake was: Were they ready to be baptized and break from the Orthodox Church, establishing a new church in Menz? Or did they want to remain in their church, at least for the time being, and work for revival and new life from within? When they looked at it that way, they had to admit that they still felt their right place was within their church. They firmly believed that as more people came to know Christ in a real way, some changes in traditions and beliefs would be made. If they were wrong, they still had the option of leaving the church.

So, they didn't participate in the Lord's Supper that day. But they watched and worshiped. They saw the service in all its beauty and simplicity. It wasn't treated as a mysterious rite reserved only for the clergy, but it was performed in the open for all to see. In addition, it wasn't limited to the very young and the very old—the only ones considered without sin in Menz. After a time of prayer and soul-searching, nearly every member of the church participated.

Our friends went back to Menz after that service with a new vision. They realized that they were part of a worldwide family bound together by Jesus' love. While they were in Addis, God had awakened in them an intense desire to share the Gospel in every way possible while there was still time.

Set Apart

While they were worshiping the Lord and fasting, the Holy Spirit said, "Set apart for me Barnabas and Saul for the work to which I have called them." So after they had fasted and prayed, they placed their hands on them and sent them off.

Acts 13:2–3

When Paul had finished speaking, he knelt down with all of them and prayed. They all wept as they embraced him and kissed him. What grieved them most was his statement that they would never see his face again. Then they accompanied him to the ship.

Acts 20:36–38

All during the spring months, the thought of our coming furlough kept haunting us. What would happen when we left? Would anyone take our place? Would the new believers continue to meet on their own? No one had been a born-again Christian longer than two and a half years. It was such a short time and there was so much to learn. Every time we talked about it we were no closer to a solution. We clung to the hope that the Lord would somehow take care of it at our last big meeting in May 1976.

They wanted to gather in Kaya this time. The tent would serve as a meeting room, and they offered to let the visitors sleep in their homes. John Cheyne was invited once more as an evangelist along with Tesfaye Workneh, one of their favorite tape preachers. Muko and his bride went along with us and completed the teaching team.

At first, we were disappointed at the small turnout. Only about eighty came and we had been hoping more of the new students would attend. But we believed that God was in control, even to the point of choosing who would be there.

Ayenachow came, walking the long way from Wuhay on a leg that no longer troubled him. He was accompanied by Minyelu, a relative from another compound of outcastes right behind the Groce's house. Minyelu began attending Bible studies at Wolde Tsadik's urging and very soon made a commitment to Christ. Without delay he began holding family devotions and teaching others in his compound.

Both Ayenachow and Minyelu were welcomed warmly by those gathered. When it came time to eat, they were included without question. At night everyone decided not to go home. Instead, they just slept on the ground in the tent, snuggling close together for warmth. Again, the outcastes were an accepted part of the group.

This meeting was different from previous ones in other ways too. They did a large part of the leading. They took turns being in charge of singing, sword drills, and prayer time. Several of them preached, and each evening was spent hearing personal testimonies of the Lord's working in their lives. The second evening, many of the students who had been uncommitted up to this point, put their trust in Christ. Most of them were from the adjoining area of Digimsha. Not all the new students we had been teaching came, but the ones who did were ready to follow the Lord's leading.

Girls also came to this meeting for the first time. They had been attending classes all during the spring months. In spite of their shyness, several of them found the courage to stand together and confess that God was speaking to their hearts. A few of them were even able to pass the test and win a Bible. God was opening the door for women through the young men we had trained.

We never forgot for long that we were in a battle and that our enemy was not people or institutions, but Satan. A young boy of about fourteen showed up during that meeting. We had never seen him before. He went straight to the front and stood beside the speaker. Then he turned to face the listening group. Hunched over with eyes that darted nervously back and forth, he seemed never to blink. He paced restlessly, his eyes always on the seated group.

When we prayed, he mumbled or even talked aloud. The things he said were weird and disjointed. Some at the meeting knew who he was. They said that he had no home and that by choice he slept right out in the middle of the meadow, with no shelter whatsoever. He was reputed to have a demon. When we talked to him, he readily admitted his strange behavior, but said he couldn't help it. Something was driving him. Whenever we talked to him about Jesus or Satan, he was evasive, always changing the subject.

Monday was the final day of the meeting. We still felt that the Lord would act in some special way to prepare for our leaving. We looked forward to the prayer and testimony time on that last evening. Response had been good the night before. As darkness fell, a young deacon asked for a chance to speak. He began telling how the Lord had convicted him of the sin of being rude and disobedient to the elders at his church, as well as to his parents. As he spoke, it was obvious that the Spirit of the Lord was stirring many hearts.

At that precise moment, a piercing voice was heard outside. Something was shouted out in an urgent tone. Almost as one body, those in the tent jumped to their feet and plunged toward the narrow exit through the rock wall at the end of the tent. Clouds of dust billowed up in the room as they stampeded out.

Our hearts hammered with fear. What was the trouble? Only a handful remained, and they couldn't answer our question. The boy who was always pacing remained beside us, rolled up in his blanket asleep. He had curled up in that position as soon as the service began, and we had decided to leave him alone. At least he wasn't bothering us. But before long he began talking in his sleep. We had been trying to decide whether to wake him when everyone left in such haste.

We waited for what seemed a very long time, and people finally began filtering back in. One told us that a woman had discovered her bull was missing, and she was anxious to recover it before it was too late. It had either been stolen or was lost out on the big grazing area. Her two sons were in the meeting, and in her anxiety, she had called on them to help. The rest just went along to see what was happening. They hadn't found the bull yet.

The previous sense of the Spirit's presence had been completely shattered. We couldn't expect anyone to hear the Lord speaking in the present tense atmosphere. We needed to pray. Bowing our heads, we took our stand against the devil as a foe defeated by the blood of Jesus and told him that he had no right to be in that tent. We prayed for the peace of God in our hearts.

Just then the mumblings of the boy in the blanket got more insistent. Some of the things he said were quite profane and vulgar. It was too much. We would have to wake him up. We jerked the blanket off his head, but instead of finding a sleeping form, we found him staring back, very much awake. Right then and there, we prayed for him. In the name of Jesus Christ, he settled down and became quiet.

One by one the students returned as we continued to pray. At the end of an hour everyone was back, and we again felt God's presence. It turned out that the bull had never left the woman's yard, but it had merely jumped the fence and was in another part. The details didn't really matter. We recognized it as one of Satan's tactics, and because we had seen it and stood against it in Jesus' name, he had fled.

All during the evening, various persons shared about the Lord's working in their lives or confessed their sins and accepted Jesus as Savior. Then, about midnight, Aschallew told us that he had something he wanted to say. He blurted out what they already knew so well, namely how mean and tough he used to be. But that was before he met Jesus.

"Now with God's help I've changed," he confided. "Drunkenness used to be such a terrible problem for me that I've solved it by stopping drinking altogether. You've seen how I haven't spent a penny of my rug profits on myself. I just don't care about material things the way I did before I gave my life to Jesus. Women and sex used to cause me lots of trouble, too, but God has delivered me from that. I still say impulsive things sometimes, but I am sorry afterward. It really makes me feel terrible when the Gospel is hindered by my behavior, because the thing I want most in life is for people to know Jesus."

"I think maybe he wants me to be a teacher like Paul and never marry," he went on. "And that's okay with me. I really love children and would like to have some of my own, but most of all I want to do His will. If I do that, I know He'll keep me happy. I have a plan that I'd like to share with you. I went to deacon school for five years in Jamaa, two days' walk from here. I know from personal experience that no one there knows the Bible. I can't get those people off my mind. I've decided to use my rug profits and buy a donkey so that I can take Bibles to them and teach them about Jesus. I have just one question. What do you think about it? Do you agree that I'm doing the right thing, or is this just my own private idea? When I go, am I going on my own, or am I going on your behalf?"

Before they could answer, Haile Giorgis jumped up. "For five years I've been here in Menz in deacon school, dreaming of the day I could go back home to Boruna," he announced. "Now the time has finally come, and I've discovered something unusual. I don't really want to go. I've come to like it here. I've found Christian brothers, and this is where my heart is."

"When I first became a Bible student of the missionaries, I was so proud of the Bible I won. I held it up on my shoulder and paraded it around for everyone to see. Now I realize that it's knowing what's inside the Bible that counts, not just owning one. I would like to just stay here, but I feel that God is calling me to go back and share with my family and friends all that I've learned. If I don't go, how will they ever hear? Will you pray for me as I take some of what we've found here and share it there?"

Then Girma raised his hand. "I think God wants me right here," he said. "I've been feeling for some time that he wants me to be a preacher. But I would like to know if God has revealed the same thing to you. Do you agree? Then, too, I would like the missionaries to pray for me before they leave."

The Lord was at last doing what we had hoped for so long He would do. But we hadn't known exactly how He would do it. He was setting apart those He had chosen for service. We asked if the Lord had spoken to anyone else.

Tatuk rose to speak. For several months he had been thinking about the future. "I believe the Lord gave a light to the Orthodox Church a long time ago," he stated. "And they have let it go out. I think it's our job to rekindle that light. I believe the Lord wants me to be a preacher, too."

God had been generous. He had called out four: two home missionaries and two pastors. At that point there was a feeling of completeness. We all talked it over and prayed about it, and everyone was in accord. They agreed that God had set these four aside for special service.

The next question asked was: where would they get the authority for what they were to do? The only power they knew of came from the *Abuna*. We referred again to our only guidebook—the Bible. When Barnabas and Saul were set apart for service, the group fasted and prayed and then laid hands on them and gave them their blessing. They concluded that the group had served as sort of a communal Pope.

We had one last service in the tent at dawn the next morning. After each of the four gave his testimony, John Cheyne reviewed the biblical basis for our actions and then anointed each one with oil. They knelt under their blankets right on the grassy stubble. Each of the believers who felt he could take a public stand of commitment, went by and laid hands on them and prayed for them. There could not have been a simpler setting for the service that morning, but I doubt that we'll ever see one that is any more beautiful.

Before taking the tent down, we took time to say goodbye to each of them. We realized that due to the political situation, there was a possibility we wouldn't be able to return to Ethiopia after our furlough. We might be saying goodbye for the last time. That made it doubly difficult. Using the traditional Ethiopian kiss of greeting on each cheek, we bid them goodbye one by one. It was one of the hardest things we have ever done. We felt like our hearts were big loaves of bread and we were tearing off hunks and parceling them out piece by piece.

Just before we left, one of them was inspired to say, "When you go to America, tell them about Jesus just like you've told us." We felt like we were being commissioned as missionaries to our own country by this little band of believers. We finally managed to get loaded and headed for home. We had only two days left in Menz, and everything had to be packed.

We made one last visit to Wolde Tsadik's compound that afternoon. He was finally back from the hospital with two good legs. He was very proud of his new appendage. Before we said goodbye, we sat down and prayed together. His father happened to be there that day, as he had been several times in the past few months. It had been several years since he had moved out and set up housekeeping near Mehal Meda. When we came, he was interested in what we were doing for Wolde Tsadik and in our craft teaching. But he was never there for our evening filmstrips or Bible studies, so we didn't expect him to really understand anything spiritual.

We were quite surprised when, after a few prayers, we heard an old man's voice break in. It had to be him. The brothers didn't sound like that. We listened as he talked to God. "Lord, You know what this house used to be like. It was a terrible place with fighting going on all the time. Everyone lived in constant fear of the *tenkway*. It was a place filled with darkness. But now I see things are different. There is a happiness and a joy that I've never known before. I feel good when I'm here. I want Jesus in my heart so that I can be like they are." When we heard that, the Lord filled us so full we thought that we would burst. Our cups were truly overflowing.

On Wednesday, we finished packing. We had hardly completed the task when at dusk fifteen friends arrived from Kaya to spend the night. They felt that they just had to say goodbye once more. The brief time after the meeting the day before simply hadn't been enough. And so, we spent our last night in Menz fellowshipping together. We had become as close to these young men as to members of our own family, and we knew we would miss them greatly.

Thursday was clinic and market day. We had our usual Bible studies, and late in the afternoon we finally left Menz. A chapter in our life closed that day, but we knew we would never forget. We were so thankful that God had allowed us to be there at exactly that time. We counted ourselves privileged for having seen, firsthand, God at work in such a remarkable way. And having seen it, we knew we would never be the same again.

Epilogue

On arriving there, they gathered the church together and reported all that God had done through them and how he had opened a door of faith to the Gentiles. And they stayed there a long time with the disciples.

Acts 14:27–28

We said goodbye to Ethiopia in June 1976. In spite of our reluctance to leave, we needed a furlough. It gave us a chance to live with our children as a family again. Also, we wanted to share about the Lord's wonderful working in Ethiopia with those in our churches in America who had so faithfully supported us and prayed for us.

All year long we watched the news of Ethiopia carefully, hoping we would be able to return when the time came. We got as far as getting our plane tickets. Then two weeks before we were to leave the United States, we were asked to wait. In less than a month, in June 1977, all our missionaries left Ethiopia.

We did not get to return to Menz until February 2003, over twenty-five years later. We were encouraged and amazed at all God had done during that time. We had left a small group of new believers. We came back to find many groups of New Testament believers scattered throughout the Amhara highlands of the province of Shoa. Everywhere we went, we found people who thanked us for planting the seed so many years ago. The harvest was greater than we had dared to dream.

For six years after we left, the new believers stayed in the Orthodox Church and witnessed to their newfound faith. It was during a time when the Marxist Communist government was in control, and they faced many hardships. In addition, they began to face great persecution by the Orthodox Church. After much soul-searching, they finally formed their own church of born-again believers.

Along with some other groups of believers who had also left the Orthodox Church, they settled on the name Addis Kidan (New Testament) for their church. They felt this best pictured their trust in Jesus as a New Testament Savior, rather than in Old Testament laws. The Addis Kidan Baptist Church was established as a denomination with three churches in 1989. In addition to the church in Menz, two churches were formed in Addis Abeba.

When famine swept Ethiopia in 1984, the Baptist Mission sent famine relief teams to remote places in the Amhara highlands to supply food. Then they sent development teams in the 1990s. Christian workers took their faith with them, and New Testament churches sprang up wherever they went. Today there are groups of believers in Bulga, Mereha Bete, Gishe Rabel, Meranya, Degolo, Sheel Afaf, Gundo Meskel, Molale, Zemero, Gin Ager, Alem Ketema, Shola Gebeya, Menjir, and Ararti, as well as other places.

People used to laugh at backward Menzies. Today the Menz believers have embraced development by the government and by World Vision. The area of Kaya is known as an evangelical place because people have given up going to the *adbar* and the *tenkway*. Women no longer have *tzars*. They don't sacrifice the *borenticha*. Now there are a number of evangelical churches in Menz, and many children of believers have done so well in school that they have gone on to university and are providing important service to Ethiopia in many ways. A number have even gone outside of Ethiopia to spread their faith in Europe and the United States. The people of Menz have truly come out of darkness into light.

Afterword

The Lord has continued to do marvelous things in Ethiopia. Addis Kidan Baptist Church was organized with three churches in 1989. Today, in 2024, there are over 350 churches and new church plants spread over the country. Pastors and church leaders are being trained on a regular basis. In the past year, 2,865 converts were baptized.

Many rural churches have kindergartens for children who have not gotten the opportunity to attend school. They are in the process of building a clinic to serve a key town in need of health care. These projects bridge the gap between people steeped in tradition and anything new. Every church is being challenged to plant another church in a nearby town that has no evangelical witness.

Lauralee with Girma and Wolde Aragay

All this is being done at the hands of the Ethiopians who make up the Addis Kidan Baptist Church denomination. They are not directed by any outside organization. They have a board of directors that guides them each step of the way. In faith, they built a seven-story office building in Addis Ababa. Each floor was added as funds became available. Now they are renting out office space on several floors to other non-profit organizations to finance the operation of the head office. They are currently in the process of building a similar office building in Debre Berhan, a city strategic to their work north of Addis Abeba.

Because they have the capacity to plan and carry out their decisions, they are trusted. A number of other nonprofit organizations are funding projects through their churches. This has helped them to grow and minister to their communities.

In addition, a nonprofit bookstore was founded in 2006 in our home in Texas. Books and magazines are sold on eBay to benefit Heart for Ethiopia. All workers are volunteers, and there are no overhead costs. Almost everything sold in the store has been donated. All profits are sent to Addis Kidan Baptist Church in Ethiopia. Over $1,500,000 has been raised so far.

The store will close at some point, since we are now in our eighties, but those leading Addis Kidan have been resourceful and have designed a way to be self-supporting. The future is bright for the Lord's work through the Addis Kidan Baptist Church.

Translation of Amharic Letters

Yekateet 10, 1969
(February 18, 1977)

May our greetings reach you through the will of Jesus Christ. In Christ you have become our teachers, brothers, and sisters. To Mr. and Mrs. Lindholm, John, Julie, and Stephen.

How have you been since the day you left us? Other than our longing for you, may our Lord, Savior, and Master, God be praised and honored, we are fine. But our longing for you has grown until it has become too much. We believe God's Spirit is with you. He is with us also. We know you are longing for us too. Let it be. God's goodness never ceases and we long and pray that you will come back to us, and we will get to see each other with our physical eyes. We are praying to that end. We have this hope and more.

Now in our country the harvest is all in. The small rains have begun and we're plowing. We heard that winter was very bad in your country with lots of rain and cold. We haven't gotten a letter from you in quite a while, but we got two letters the month before. We think you'll soon write to us.

There is much spiritual awakening around us. There are many students and praise God we are still having lessons at Girma's. Each Sunday at church, Girma and Tatuk have been permitted to preach. The people are listening patiently. But they are also watching our lives very carefully. We are afraid lest we become stumbling blocks. We think you are already praying for us.

Abba Asefa has become the leader of the Akafee Mikael Church. Because he is our friend and we help him, he has commanded that the gospel be preached on Sundays. Therefore, we are preaching in love. Abba Asefa is really lonesome for you. He begs you to write him and pray for him.

Doctor Jerry, Mr. Groce, and Doctor Muko sometimes take turns coming to teach us. There are some very strong students. So many people are asking where the Lindholms went. "They are in their country, and they'll return," we tell them.

We haven't gotten any news or letter from Haile Giorgis. Nothing has reached us. If he has sent you a letter, send it on to us. We are going ahead and praying for him, even though we don't know anything about him.

Aschallew didn't move away in June. He went one time and returned. He hasn't been since then and we don't understand why. He's a little afraid. May God's will be done rather than man's. We don't feel God's will has been fulfilled yet.

We were very happy because a new missionary came from America to Ethiopia in January. We have hopes he will teach us in the future.

We haven't yet gone from our area to any other. In other words, we have just been teaching in our own vicinity. But we don't know where God will take us in the future. We are only praying that we follow His will.

And we know that God causes all things to work together for good for those who love God, to those who are called according to His purpose (Romans 8:28).

Be anxious for nothing, but in everything by prayer and supplication with thanksgiving let your requests be made known to God. And the peace of God, which surpasses all comprehension, shall guard your hearts and your minds in Christ Jesus (Philippians 4:6–7).

We are only praying that Jesus leads our hearts and thoughts in His will only, and that we won't be separated from His care.

"Remember also your Creator in the days of your youth, before the evil days come and the years draw near when you will say, 'I have no delight in them,'" wrote Solomon in Ecclesiastes 12:1. Having made this a guide for our lives, we continue on.

Please help us by your prayers as we help you. I can do all things through Christ who strengthens me (Philippians 4:13). Amen.

To our teachers, Mr. and Mrs. Lindholm. To our brothers and sister, John, Julie, and Stephen. May God's grace be with you. Amen.

Sent from all Kaya students
By Tatek Kebede and Girma Biru

27 Sinay 1969
(4 July 1977)

Since the four believers I wrote you about, thirty-seven more Moslems have turned to the Christian faith. This all happened because of your prayers. In Wulicha Saint George Church, the spread of the Gospel has made me very happy, and I know it makes you happy too. I, by God's power, am fine. Bible studies are continuing to expand.

Your spiritual brother,
Haile Giorgis

Glossary

adbar	An evil spirit associated with a particular location.
amudgway	Name of a large community grazing area.
arekay	A strong distilled liquor.
Ato	Mr.
Baite Kahinet	The official legal and administrative arm of the Orthodox Church.
borenticha	A black sheep sacrificed to appease Satan.
budda	An evil eye, either of a person or the sun.
chelay	An amulet or charm for protection.
Derg	Ruling body during the revolultion.
doola	A combination walking stick and club.
dubtera	The highest-ranking church leader on the theological or educational level—frequently a powerful wizard.
Felasha	An outcaste who claims Jewish ancestry. Also known as *Beta Israel*—House of Israel today.
gabi	A heavy white cotton shawl.
gared	A servant girl.
injera	A large, sour, spongy pancake that is the main diet staple.
tezcar	A ceremonial meal at church in honor of someone who has died.

tenkway	A wizard who is usually also a church priest.
tella	A local drink made from fermented grain.
Timket	An Orthodox holiday celebrating Christ's baptism.
tzar	A demon given to a person on request from a *tenkway*.